LIBRARY

The Coaching Parent

St. Patrick's School

The Coaching Parent

David Miskimin and Jack Stewart

Typeset in Garamond

Praise for The Coaching Parent

"The Coaching Parent is a really innovative approach which allows parents and children to deal with difficult situations in a constructive and positive way in the home environment."

Don McLaverty
Parent with two children

"However experienced, capable and sensitive we may be when dealing with adults or other young people, it is always far more difficult to present a calm approach when endeavouring to encourage and help our own children. The emotions present in such close relationships often make our comments appear as criticisms or of us as having over–demanding expectations. It is therefore invaluable to have The Coaching Parent as a resource that suggests practical examples and strategies which we parents can employ as we lovingly prepare our children to tackle and achieve greater challenges with flair and success."

Joy Naylor
Vocal Coach and a parent with L plates on!

"As a business consultant and Mum to two lively boys aged 9 and 7, The Coaching Parent is universally an essential read and source of reference. My 2 boys' personalities are so different that it is essential that I can build rapport with each of them, question and listen to uncover their personal issues, praise according to what has meaning to them and deal with their diverse self–confidence issues. With the skills and techniques in the book I can "coach" each of my boys so much better. Additionally I can now use the newly acquired techniques with my clients and the teams they have to manage."

Annette R. Kurer
Ark Consultants – consultancy, coaching and training

"I have used the concepts in The Coaching Parent and found them to be invaluable. Coaching your child opens up new areas of development for both of you."

Mother with two children

"This book provides the encouragement, inspiration and the practical tools needed to help you tackle the most challenging job on the planet – being a parent."

Paul McGee
Author of the best selling book 'S.U.M.O... Shut Up, Move On.'

"The Coaching Parent arrived into my life on my 52nd birthday and as I began to read the philosophy and ideas expounded by David and Jack, I realised that I have never read a single book about parenting, attended a lecture, watched or listened to anything.

"Yet I have co-parented 5 children whom I am proud to describe as some of my best friends. Like the best of friends, we occasionally have our spats and 'don't call each other enough' and yet, when the chips are down, we are there for each other — unconditionally.

"I reflect that, maybe part of my 'success' as a parent has been facilitated by my career as a business coach — and by the books, conferences and people I have met in the development of my coaching skills.

"Somebody is quoted as saying that 'parenting is the last great preserve of the amateur'.

"I don't know whether I would have made a better job of it if The Coaching Parent had been around 19 years ago when all of this began but I do know that I would have felt less lonely, less inadequate and less fearful of the outcome of this perilous journey."

Chris Barrow
Principal of The Dental Business School, The Coaching
Business School and The Online Business School

"We found it really easy to get to grips with the flow of the book and the advice provided from the cards. It has endorsed our 25 years practical experience of being parents, and certainly provided us with many different ideas to assist in the coaching of our grandson. It also makes sense of many of the challenges that we faced with our children. It's a pity this book was not available all those years ago when they were growing up."

Steve and Lynn Bugg
Parents with two children

"The Coaching Parent isn't just a simple system that works; it acknowledges that parenting is work and shows you how to do that work properly. It causes you to lift your game and reach new levels of relationships with your children."

Nikki and Mike
Parents with two children

"The Coaching Parent fills a significant gap in coaching literature. Most coaches come from a sports, business, education or psychology background and focus their work on those fields. Surely many of them are parents too and this is where coaching should start. The Coaching Parent is a resource for parents who care - like all parents. I was especially gratified to discover how much importance and space is given to the building of self-confidence in all its forms. This is the foundation stone for life and needs to be set early. Who better to do it than parents, and here is how."

Sir John Whitmore, best selling author of 'Coaching for Performance: Growing People, Performance and Purpose.'

"As a parent, early years teacher, school governor and someone who has benefited from coaching; I know that coaching helps to build self esteem, break down barriers and release latent potential. It explores and develops the skills necessary to do this in a way that is relevant to each individual, recognising the fact that children and adults learn in many different ways. It helps individuals to reach and achieve their maximum potential whilst also developing invaluable life skills. I think this book would be a valuable resource not only in every parent's library, but also for anyone interested in improving and developing learning skills."

Gail Steele

"You carry your precious child for 9 months but nothing can prepare you for the enormity of the responsibility until the birth. For weeks after my son's birth I felt that I had misplaced the much needed 'handbook' which would tell me what to do and which I so desperately needed. Eight months later I feel a little more confident but recognise that at every junction the decisions my husband and I make could impact upon our son's life and development. The Coaching Parent is the handbook which I have been looking for, allowing my family to develop in a positive way without imposing strict rules that we all have to adhere to."

Natasha Jones
Mother and Practice Partner CFP Solicitors

"Train up a child in the way he should go: and when he is old, he will not depart from it"

Proverbs 22:6

Acknowledgements

One of my core beliefs is that "Everything counts". Whatever we do or don't do, has an effect. So with reference to inspiration and material for this work, there are multiple sources. If you feel aggrieved that your name is not mentioned, I hope you are able to forgive me.

I failed my 11 plus and my teachers led a lengthy inquest as to how it could happen! My best friend just scraped in to Grammar School and much to our shared dismay, we were parted. I know he won't mind me saying that for several years he struggled near the bottom of his classes, while I was always in the top 3 for most of mine. I was already learning that 'failure' is down to how we interpret the experience. Mr Comrie inspired me as a teacher, where he demonstrated without using the words, that goals and expectation of outcome are powerful motivators. My final GCE exam result was precisely as he predicted.

My parents, brother John and sister Karen, have provided a source of ideas and reference; like me, always doing the best with what they knew. Friends and wider family, especially the greatly loved and sorely missed Ken Mason, played their part too, with much wisdom and support over the years. My wife Laura has believed in me throughout and contributed much to my growth as a parent, husband and coach. Our daughters Nicole and Anne–Marie have (usually) been willing students, and where necessary, adept in letting me know when I get it wrong! Grandchildren Marcus and Aiden, continue to both remind and inform me about how adults and children interact in the real world!

Achieving a personal goal of meeting 1:1 with Lou Tice, International Consultant on Personal Motivation and co–founder of *The Pacific Institute*, was a deeply moving and life changing event. "Thank you Lou – you are one in a million."

My big secret is out – while over the years several hundred coaching clients have produced fabulous results, I too have experienced a sense of achievement and growth by sharing in their hard won personal change.

Speaking of which, thanks Jack for coming into my life at just the right time. Working with you on this book has been an experience I would not have wanted to miss. In turns; exciting, frustrating, fun, annoying, enlightening, disappointing and ultimately, fulfilling. I can't think of anyone else who would have matched my needs better!

Finally, as authors with experience of different publishers, we both wanted to acknowledge Bookshaker.com. Flexibility, creativity, professionalism, tireless efforts – let's limit the superlatives as others might think Debbie Jenkins and Joe Gregory wrote them – we mean it – well done guys, great work!

God bless those who have contributed in my journey through life.

David Miskimin

Just about everyone who I value, and many of those who I don't yet, influences me, so below are those most relevant to this book.

My own wonderful parents, now departed, who in keeping my adoption secret, taught me the power of love. I am forever grateful to my brilliant wife, Anne, who continues the lesson. To my step–daughters Karen and Janet, both model parents themselves.

Bob Szpalek, headteacher in a million, and his students at Darlaston Community School. Mark Leeson, Malcolm Ratledge, and Theresa Powney, educationalists. Keith Greenwood and Chris Wolfenden, who gave us a break to work with parents of their excellent school.

Tim and Carol Howard, who opened the door at Walsall LEA. To the support proved by Len Blood, Nick Poole and my Purrfect business partner, Jeff Moran.

And finally, all the NLP trainers, who continue to make the world a better place: Frank Bentley, Peter McNab, Robert McDonald, Steve and Connirae Andreas, Penny Tompkins and James Lawley.

Like David, I have mixed views about 'success' and 'failure' in education, and despite my probably having too many qualifications, two incredible teachers helped lift me back on the rails in the late 60's, Eric Liddle and 'Charlie' Parker.

The warmth and sincerity of David Miskimin has always shone through from day one. Typically, he persuaded me, a lifelong Liverpool supporter to read Alex Ferguson's book, 'Managing My Life'! World–class rapport skills from a wonderful human being.

Jack Stewart

Contents

Foreword

As a coach and someone who has been a trainer of coaches for many years I am honoured by the opportunity to work with thousands of coaches and students from all around the world. There is enormous gratification in hearing feedback from them that tells me something important – that coaching works.

I like to think that I have been relatively successful in business but of course there is more to life than just work. In addition to my business, I have the pleasure of being the proud father of three boys. Yet with all my 'skills' and experience nothing prepared me adequately for becoming a parent.

Nobody can quite prepare you for the enormous changes that take place. It was so different when my wife and I were just a couple. Then we had our first child, and when he was a baby things were absolutely fine, but then he started to walk, talk and develop a personality and my goodness things did change! The whole dynamics of the family changes, the relationships become far more complicated and there is so much more to think about and deal with. Now I have three children, all boys: a 15 year–old, a 13 year–old and a 6 year–old. One might be forgiven for thinking that having had one child it makes little difference if you have more – after all you have learned all about it now. How wrong! The beauty of children is that they are so unique and this of course means that what worked for one is completely useless with another. You are constantly trying to deal with very different personalities whilst trying to maintain a family unity.

The major difference between being a parent and running a business is that when you encounter a challenge or problem in business and you successfully deal with it, you are then able to put into place processes and systems to ensure that you never meet the same problem again. This of course is absolutely not true in parenting.

Over the years, I have heard the phrase "good parenting" many times. A phrase that is talked about all the time and is absolutely guaranteed to make those of us who are parents feel guilty, inadequate and insecure.

However, the good news is I did not have to look very far for help. I soon realised that the techniques I employed with my clients as a coach could be of immense use to me as a parent.

So what is coaching? Well here is my definition:

"Coaching is about performing at your best through the individual and private assistance of someone who will challenge, stimulate and guide you to keep growing."

Explained more fully, your coach engages in a collaborative alliance with you to establish and clarify purpose and goals and to develop a plan of action to achieve those goals. They will establish an understanding of what is really important to you in life and subsequently enable you to take charge of your life; to construct and act upon action plans that will help you to realise these priorities.

Coaching also incorporates learning, and yet a coach is not a teacher and will not necessarily know how to do things better than you but this does not matter. Your coach will observe patterns – set the stage for new actions and then work with you to put these new, more successful actions into place. This involves learning through various coaching techniques such as listening, reflecting, asking questions and providing information. Finally, and most importantly, your coach will help you learn how to become self–correcting and self–generating. That is, you will learn how to correct your own behaviour, generate your own questions and find your own answers.

So if you think about it, isn't this precisely what we do with our children?

I have personally known David Miskimin for many years as both a fellow coach and a friend. During that time, not only have I witnessed him coach many other people, but have also experienced his coaching myself. David really is a master of the Art; I have seen him work with people and in a short space of time completely reframe their thinking and help them go through a process of cognitive restructuring such that their emotional state changed very quickly indeed. As a coach I have the highest respect for him and his ability, and as a friend I count myself honoured to be able to call on his coaching skills to help me in my times of need as indeed I have had occasion to do in the past.

Whilst I have not met Jack personally, his passion for giving children the opportunity to improve their life chances is evident. His skills and experience with youngsters, and David's extensive coaching background, have uniquely blended to create something really special in this work.

When I received the first draft of this book it was with such relief that I found it answered many questions that I have, not just as a father but as a coach and trainer of coaches. It placated many of my own fears and managed to cover this in–depth subject in such a quiet, caring, calm and easy to understand way. This book is most definitely required reading and must have a permanent place of residence on the bedside table of any would be father or mother.

Gerard O'Donovan
Founder and Principal of Noble Manhattan Coaching
CEO of the European Coaching Institute

Introduction

The path of parenting is strewn with potholes and traps as any parent will tell you. Yet, in spite of the pain, anxiety and frustration, we continue. Parents love their children – so we persist. There is also that nagging part of us, working hard in some way to give our child more hope, skills, and possibility for their lives than we had in ours. It's not that we have failed or under performed, more that there is a part of us – maybe its called wisdom or experience – demanding to be heard. Sometimes voiced or played as a thought perhaps like "Knowing what I do now, I'd do it this way…"

With the pressures of modern life including long or unsocial working hours, family break–up is reaching crisis levels. Whatever your own circumstances, and with stability or not, any child in your care remains important to you. As parents we need all the help we can get. Not for our sakes, but for the children.

This book provides many resources for you to reach into in whatever way is best for you. By experimenting and practicing with the tools, techniques and knowledge in this book, you will very quickly find yourself becoming a coach.

Finally, please remember – however you approach this as *The Coaching Parent* – always do it with love.

David and Jack

The World's Best Coach ...

Imagine you could afford the world's best coach for your child. Watch, listen to and feel what it is like as your child blossoms, discovers hidden talents and abilities, and develops an ever–deepening level of *self–confidence*. Notice how the coach is working. Marvel at the wonderful *rapport* coach and child share, how *learning* has become not only enjoyable, but also easier and faster. Stress? The *coaching relationship* even helps your child to *use 'stress' to their advantage*, applying their newly discovered responsibility to make rapid strides towards realising their potential. How much would you give to employ this person?

Well, imagine now *you* are that coach. Watch, listen to and feel what it is like as you work with your child, doing everything the coach did, and more! Adjust the script; as in your mind's eye you combine the deep love and respect you have for your child, with the skills of the world's best coach. Notice the absence of any barriers to achievement for both of you…

And the next step? Welcome to **The Coaching Parent!** You are now on your way to becoming your child's personal, inspirational coach.

This book will make *you* the world's best coach for your child. All the tools and motivation you need to *make the best use of the coaching opportunities that arise daily* are in these pages. Depending on your style, needs and experience you can dip into whichever chapter appeals most. Alternatively, you can start your journey right now and read the book from cover to cover. It really is up to you.

CHAPTER ONE

Taking your first steps

Exactly what is *coaching?*

Coaching is a term now commonly heard in sports, business and education. We realise this does not automatically mean that you, the reader, necessarily appreciate all the similarities or differences. We felt that a brief explanation might be helpful, so that the coaching style we propose for *The Coaching Parent* can be more easily understood.

In many ways, developing a coaching relationship with a child has perhaps the closest parallels to sports coaching. However, unlike sports coaching, we are not helping our child prepare for a win/lose competition. Our approach, is focused on a collaborative win/win result, which will enable your child to grow as an individual rather than to beat their "opponent."

In sports, the coach can rarely outperform those coached. Some of our most successful sports coaches never achieved the highest levels in their chosen sport. Maybe there is a link with us acting as parents? As a parent or step–parent many of us can experience self–doubt. Many of us struggle with:

- "Am I getting this right?"

- "Is this the best thing to do with my child in this situation?"

- "That parent seems to have a better relationship that I do."

- "I'll never be a good parent."

Dilemmas like these are especially strong when it's a first child we are dealing with. In business the coach will probably be an accomplished 'player'. For example is it possible to conceive of a successful sales manager who was never a salesperson? Yet, we as the parent have never 'been there' with many situations we face with our child. In sports, coaching is a full–time job supported in many cases with assistant coaches. For the parent it's a bit like having a husband, partner, relative or best friend to support you. Other times, you will need to move forward on your own.

We know the coach has many diverse responsibilities. In gymnastics, for example, the coach usually works one–on–one. Many sports coaches see themselves primarily as teachers. In business, even though the word "coach" has become a popular addition to most managers' job descriptions, it's doubtful that the word "teacher" would also appear.

The role of the parent in any child interaction varies in its importance based on many factors – try substituting 'parent' for 'coach' in the next few sentences. For example some research[1] indicates younger childrens' perceptions of the performance qualities of other athletes are influenced as much by a coach's reaction as their own opinions. In older age–groups young adolescents' personal decisions are more influential than a coach's reactions.

When Jack and I [David] discovered we shared a common area in which we both felt passionate, it was a revelation. He had spent much of his life working with children, removing blocks to their learning and development. In his opinion, this was an area in which a difference desperately needed to be made. His aim was to explain and demonstrate that children can learn quicker and remember more, enjoy the delights of

---

[1] *Amorose, A. J., & Weiss, M. R. (1998). Coaching feedback as a source of information about perceptions of ability: A developmental examination. *Journal of Sport and Exercise Psychology, 20,* 395–420.

being truly listened to, reduce their stress levels, and become even more confident. He had even spoken at education conferences ensuring that his strength of views and ideas, which were not always supported by the system, were conveyed.

I had similar yet different motives. I'm very proud of the achievements of my children. However, like most parents, I wished that I'd had greater knowledge, experience and skills earlier so that I could have been even more effective in helping my children fulfil their potential. I had established a successful business career, which grew into my own executive and business coaching company.

Now, through coaching business executives, I can see the common threads between coaching in organisations and parenting. Many leaders and managers lack credibility with colleagues. If you wonder how that's relevant, ask yourself how credible are you with your children? Some bosses say one thing and do another – staff really hate that don't they? Has that ever happened in your home? A good manager will want to develop and grow individuals so that their talent and career aspirations are realised. As a result, the manager feels a sense of achievement and the individual also experiences great satisfaction. Isn't this what a parent most deeply desires for their child? Is it possible that by improving your parenting skills you may also become a better manager at work and your children learn valuable work/life skills?

While we share some beliefs and differ in others, Jack and I are convinced that God brought us together, with our different talents, to develop this programme, working with gifted, able and 'difficult' adults and children of all ages. One of our aims in this book, and beyond, is to help raise your own awareness as to your role in positively influencing your child.

HOW DOES COACHING WORK?

Coaching is a way of asking questions that empowers the listener. By asking questions, we present options and possibilities. In so doing, our awareness and understanding are likely to increase. Whomever you coach will become massively more aware of who they are, what they know, and how they function.

How much more effective would you be if you could choose the time and place to be your best, you knew why you operated as you did, and you always felt a connection to those closest to you, or your purpose, mission or calling?

Well, you can have all this, and then, as if by magic, so will your child. You will become an inspiring role model, allowing your children to copy qualities and techniques you possess that will transform their lives.

And when you are ready, maybe you can create other opportunities to use your coaching skills…

If you want to start on the journey to becoming the world's best coach for your child, consider how you might already be using daily opportunities for coaching.

How often do you catch your child doing something right, and reward them with a smile, praise, or a well–considered question?

"That's great Josh/Jessica – How good do you want to become?"

So, we begin with coaching conversations in Chapter 2. You will soon discover the 'magic' of coaching is:

1. Creating a favourable climate for dialogue

2. Using 'normal' daily opportunities

3. Having an intent to coach

4. Putting a little more thought into what you say before you say it

5.   Using questions instead of opinion

6.   Ensuring agreed actions are taken and monitored.

These coaching conversations are repeated and analysed in Chapter 12 with commentary, showing what is really 'going on.' In a very short time, the 'commentary' will be in your mind, as you seamlessly help your child realise their potential.

Just as important as how you construct your **questions** is the ability to **listen** actively. Tips and techniques on both are in Chapter 3.

By the time you have read the first three chapters, you are likely to have questions yourself! It that's the case, go to the Appendix for Frequently Asked Questions. Chapter 4 introduces a very simple yet powerful 'model' of coaching, which you will soon be using effortlessly. This model [GROW] helps with **goal** setting, becoming aware of your child's **reality**, helping them recognise additional **options**, and then choosing their own **way forward.**

The book is based on 45 'cards', each allocated into one of six suits.

1.   Rapport

2.   Self Confidence

3.   Accelerating & Improving Learning

4.   Coaching

5.   Optimising Stress

6.   Jokers

Each of these 'suits' contains key aspects of **The Coaching Parent**.

They are covered in depth in Chapters 5 through to 10. Here's a sneak preview:

1. Rapport

Rapport is a term describing the effect of all simultaneous communication between you and your child. That's verbal, non–verbal, what you notice, and what you don't. Signs that confirm the message or suggest it may be suspect are mismatches between *what* is said, and *how* it is said revealed by posture, tone, gestures and facial expression. These external signals are far more reliable than guesswork or intuition. However, intuition i.e. 'this doesn't feel right', has the potential to be your best indicator, if you are skilled at using it, and when it is combined with the tools you are about to learn.

Without rapport, you cannot influence anyone, unless you use coercive force. We know you love your child. Yet in loving him or her, you may have overlooked simple yet very important things like your body language, tone of voice and physical position in relation to them. Here you will explore a collection of thinking, life skills and life stories that are obvious only *after* you have learned them! Develop powerful links into how you and your child relate to each other and how you relate to the world. Being 'in rapport' means communication flows effortlessly, without prejudice or barriers. It is like a dance between equal partners, each trusting each other, each movement occurring almost telepathically.

2. Self Confidence

The most limiting thing we can have is the lack of belief in ourselves. How we think about ourselves and how we present ourselves to the world hugely influences how far we get in life. Many now famous people in history used self–belief to conquer massive obstacles. Their parents, teachers, or employers wrote many of them off originally. You will discover how so much of how you think and what you think about is tied closely into your self–confidence. Real confidence radiates out and lifts others. False or low confidence does the opposite.

3. Accelerating and Improving Learning

Are you in rapport, feeling confident? Brilliant! Now find out how you can learn more *and* remember more? Read about and then apply new learning techniques and approaches; experiment with the ideas for yourself and children.

4. Coaching

You know that coaching empowers others. Although they may adopt a different approach, think about all the great coaches in sport. How about coaches who transform people who were labelled 'tone deaf' into recording artists? But no coach, no matter how good, can perform or take exams for his or her protégés! By raising awareness and responsibility in your child, they can 'go solo', reaching heights previously undreamed of.

5. Optimising Stress

You are in rapport, confident, your learning skills honed like radar. You know and accept yourself. You want to succeed and are on your way. Now is the time to use stress to your own advantage. Stress is natural. We read and hear so much about the increase in stress these days, don't we? Set aside time to reflect on those areas of our lives where making lasting changes will benefit us forever.

6. Jokers

Who inspired you as a child? As well as your mum or dad, didn't you learn from true–life stories and collected wisdom? Share your discoveries with your children. Maybe ask them what or who it makes them think of. Could *your story* become part of our programme? All stories stimulate the right hand side of the brain, neglected in formal education. Maybe your child would like more stories to read…

IS ALL THIS BEGINNING TO MAKE SENSE?

Our aim in this book is for coaching to reach parents and children regardless of whether they're a man or a woman, a boy or a girl. With this in mind we'll aim to refer to the child as a girl and a boy equally to make things fair and the reading easier.

How many times have you wondered, "I wish I could be like her", "She inspires me", "My mum or dad might have taught me that", and "How can I be so that my child copies my best points, and forgives my worst?"

Every 'card' in this book contains skills and wisdom for life. Coaching is the missing ingredient that makes all this come to life.

You can be like *your* role models, inspire your child, and teach your child your best 'stuff' by becoming the best role model for them! This book will show you how.

We present real life examples of how coaching has helped children in Chapter 11.

In addition, as promised, in Chapter 12, we return to the coaching conversations we started with in Chapter 2.

The book closes in telling you a little about us, and recommends some further reading, tools and resources to build on your skills as *The Coaching Parent.*

Before, during and after using these materials, who do you think might be the world's best coach for you…?

CHAPTER TWO

Coaching Conversations

Are you ready to get started? Read these conversations, which we have designed to illustrate the key topics of rapport, learning, self–confidence and stress. Place yourself first in the position of the parent, then re–read them, as if you were the child. See Card 17 in *Chapter 7: Learning.*

'Coaching conversations' you have had, and will have, are more likely to cover different topics, as you will find in the Appendix – Frequently Asked Questions. However it will soon become apparent that the key issues we have addressed in *The Coaching Parent* are behind just about everything.

Remember that one definition of coaching is: "A participative partnership designed to develop an individual to their full potential."

We encourage you to seek, listen for, and grab those partnership opportunities as they present themselves.

At the end of several chapters we have inserted exercises for you to note what you've taken out of the reading. Coaching involves committing to action to achieve results and we'll be asking you to record those items too.

As a way of demonstrating how ordinary conversations can easily incorporate coaching we invite you to read the conversations below. As the book unfolds the approach taken will be revealed to you.

How might you use these conversations to help you become a better coach?

CONVERSATION 1

Dialogue between Josh [in italics] and his mum.

Mum, why is it sometimes easier to get on with Dad than at other times?

What do you mean Josh?

Well there was a problem yesterday, didn't he tell you?

No – go on …

Dad told me off for dropping my dinner off the tray.

So you lost rapport?

Rap–what? What's that?

Sorry, yes it is a strange word isn't it? Well – let me put it another way – how do you know when you are getting on with someone?

Don't know – it just sort of clicks I guess.

So when Dad told you off what was it like ?

Awful. He shouted, which I didn't like. Then he swore, which made it even worse as he never swears. Not only that, but the carpet was a horrible spaghetti Bolognese colour!

…then what happened

I said sorry – it was an accident. He wasn't happy though and made me clean it all up. He was grumpy for ages.

Later on I asked if he wanted a cup of tea and he was a lot nicer – like normal really.

How could you tell?

He smiled and he said "come here" and gave me a cuddle. He was okay after that.

So you were back in rapport?

If that's what that word means, yes I guess so. It seemed more comfortable, almost as though it had never happened. Is that what rapport is then?

That's exactly what rapport is like.

If something like this ever happened again, and I hope it doesn't, what might you do differently?

I'd apologise straight away – then say don't be cross with me for ages, as I feel uncomfortable when you do that.

How would dad take that do you think?

Don't know – he might be alright, he might not.

What could you do to find out?

I could ask him before it happens, so that he knows I don't like it!!

Interesting idea, when would you do that?

Tonight – but before tea!

How will you know if he's happy with that?

If he is understanding, then I'll know I've cracked it!

CONVERSATION 2

Jessica *[in italics]* is talking to her mum.

Mum, why am I so clumsy all the time?

What have you done Jessica…?

I've just knocked my homework books on the floor. Yesterday I knocked a cup over!

Just because you did that doesn't mean you are clumsy does it?

Well I think it does!

Jessica, it is likely if you keep insisting that you are clumsy, that soon you are going to believe it.

What do you mean?

Well – just for fun, can you imagine what the very opposite of clumsy might be?

Don't know – how about not clumsy?

Well that's true, actually I'm wondering if there is a positive way of saying that? At the moment you are saying **you're not** something. How about **I am** something…

Don't know what the opposite is – how about graceful? No that's not me either!

Okay, let's try going with that just as an experiment. How would you feel if you were graceful?

Confident I guess.

And if you were confident, how would that be?

Good!

Does a confident person ever knock her books or drinks over?

I wouldn't think so, and even if they did they probably wouldn't worry about it.

Well why don't you try that. In your mind's eye imagine you are that confident person – how is that?

…Its cool. I'm aware of everything around me. Yet, it's all under control.

How good is that?

It's great – I'm really confident.

Great stuff – just remember this moment, as you go on from here – whatever happens you are that confident person!

Thanks Mum – you're a star!

CONVERSATION 3

Josh *[in italics]* is talking to his dad.

How's it going Josh?

Terrible, I'm just rubbish at maths

Surely you can't be rubbish at all of maths, is there anything in particular that's difficult?

Well I guess its algebra mostly. We've been doing it for weeks now and I just can't get the hang of it.

What's happening with algebra then?

It just doesn't make sense at all.

Is there any of it that does make sense?

I think I know how simple equations work.

Anything else?

No that's about it, I can't do quadratics though.

How do you want to be at algebra?

I need to understand quadratics.

And if you did, what would be happening?

I'd be getting good marks.

What are your marks like now?

I get about 40% right.

Well you must be doing something right then!

15

Suppose so.

What sort of marks would you be happy with?

I'd like to get at least 70% right.

I wonder what you might do to improve – have you any ideas?

Not really.

Well to be honest maths wasn't a strong point for me either.

However I do know something about working these sort of things out.

If you were being really creative, like you are with English what sort of ideas would you come up with?

Hmmm. Well I could ask to sit with David, he seems to understand this stuff. I could ask Sir if he would give me a hand, I don't like asking in front of the others though. And I could ask for some old maths papers to practice with.

Great stuff – which of those do you prefer?

I think sitting with David, he is really good, but I don't think he'll mind helping me a little bit.

Okay – when will you sort that out?

Tomorrow I'm going to ask Chloe – she's his sister – to have a word with him because she knows him really well and she likes me!

CONVERSATION 4

Emily *[in italics]* talking to her mum.

Hi Emily, how are you?

Don't ask!

Give me an idea, I might be able to help.

Doubt it…

Shall I start guessing or will you give me an idea?

Knowing you, if I don't give you an idea, you are just going to nag me to death.

Don't be silly – go on, I'm listening…

It's Becky.

What about her?

She is such a pain, I'm sick of her, she drives me mad!

How does she do that?

Whatever I say she says, whatever I wear she wears, wherever I go she goes – I want to strangle her!

Is there a reason she does this?

No she is just stupid and it stresses me out.

I'm wondering if there might be a reason and it's just that we don't know it yet.

I don't care and what's it got to do with you anyway?

It seems to me that if you didn't care, you wouldn't be getting so stressed out.

Maybe, maybe not.

How would you like things to be with Becky?

I'd like her to go away, so that I don't feel so stressed.

Does she know that?

Not really, I just ignore her.

How do you think that makes her feel?

Probably pretty bad I guess — it's her own fault though.

Do you really want her to go away?

I do if she keeps being so stupid.

What do you think she wants?

I've no idea and I don't really care.

How could you find out?

Oh! I suppose I could ask her.

Just supposing that you did, what might be good about that?

She might tell me why she is being such a pain…

Anything else?

I would probably feel a little better just knowing why she is driving me so crazy!

We started by wanting to reduce your stress — I get the idea that talking to Becky would be worthwhile, what do you think?

Oh you drive me mad too — of course it makes sense. Thanks Mum!

Will you sort it soon?

Yes, I'll talk to her — and you — tomorrow. Are you happy now?

That's the end of the four coaching conversations. Depending on how curious you are feeling right now, you might continue your reading with the next chapter, or you might dip into Chapter 12 – Worked Examples.

CHAPTER THREE

Questioning and Listening

Questioning and listening are central to your role as you are becoming a Coaching Parent. There are some clues to be aware of which will help in knowing if it is a genuine interaction:

Both of you feel you're being heard and understood. Adult and child are open with each other.

The best aspects of communication are multi–directional, or at least it is a real two–way experience, when you and your child are both occupied with the conversation and interested.

The mood is comfortable and so the important things are said, even if the subject matter is awkward or difficult.

As a result of talking, something useful or satisfying happens and you feel good, maybe even experience an increased bond.

The above aspects apply in all forms of effective communication.

Getting the above four things right will lead to effective interactions with the following beneficial outcomes:

- You will have improved communications
- You will have better personal relationships

- You will handle difficult communication with ease

- Whatever your definition of success, you will have more of it

- You will have a great deal of fun and personal satisfaction, through effective communication.

Good communications will usually eliminate or at least minimise any possible misunderstanding of your intentions. In addition, it is likely to lead to much more involvement from your child.

QUESTIONING

Questioning is an important feature of all coaching models.

The approach of effective questioning is to ensure the child gives a detailed, non–judgmental descriptive response. By taking this approach they are less likely to end up blaming others and more likely to take greater personal responsibility. The act of describing to the parent ensures the child is also describing to himself or herself, something that until that point may have been unconscious. So awareness, followed potentially by responsibility and ownership are raised. Relevant feedback *from within* is essential for your child's continuous improvement. We will only achieve this objective by careful consideration to the construction and style of our questions.

It is worth reviewing the types of questions that may be posed:

- Closed Questions

- Incisive Questions

- Open Questions

First, think about the result you are seeking and then plan your question style according to that intended outcome.

Closed Questions

A closed question will solicit a small amount of information, even a one–word answer. A close–ended question provides agreement, contradiction, or short burst information.

Answer will usually be yes/no. *"Did you tell your teacher she would receive the report from you by this Friday latest?"* and *"Have you decided what to do about it?"*

Incisive Questions

Incisive questions are a particular type of invitation that will be extremely useful to help your child get past beliefs that are **limiting** their potential. Such questions are often called presuppositions as they 'presuppose' certain ideas in their construction. Sometimes barriers to your questions will be erected consciously, other times unconsciously. Either way this is often a useful questioning approach.

An incisive question has 2 parts:

- the first part by–passes the belief

- the second part invites new thinking beyond the belief as if it were gone

Here's an example

- And if time was not an issue …

- …then what would you do?

The only way your child can answer is to:

- Consider the situation as if the belief were no longer a constraint (i.e. it is *no longer* about time) and

- Consider the situation may have other potential solutions (i.e. they are now enabled to consider doing *something*).

While the above questions styles are both valid and useful, we have found from experience that Open Questions will most often serve you best as a Coaching Parent.

Open Questions

How, What, Where, When, Who, Why, Where, Tell me about…

An open question will usually solicit large and broad amounts of information. Starting questions with *What, When, How, Where,* or *Who* will each prompt different type of responses depending on your use. Some may be single word responses. Others will be much longer. The first question below may give a fairly short response, the second leads to a longer response.

1. How do you think the boys managed to run so fast in the 100m?

2. What types of materials are used in that painting and why those do you imagine?

Consider what sort of responses might occur with the following questions:

- What's happening at the moment in more detail?

- How worried about it are you?

- Who knows whether you want to do something about it?

- How much control do you have over the result?

- What steps have you taken on it so far?

- What has stopped you from doing more?

- What obstacles are in your way that prevent you from moving forward?

- What is really the issue here?

To go a little deeper with your questioning and the level of response from your child perhaps ask:

- What are you learning from me asking you these questions?

- How can you benefit from me asking you questions?

Be prepared for some interesting answers.

Using '*Why*' as our question preface can invoke a pushback as it may intimidate – for some it is a threatening question. It also triggers the logical part of our brain (the left side) and may lead to a justification of the response and almost a closed response – "Why? I just did, that's why!" The alternative question prefaces tend to cause a right brain response and often offer more insight and emotional clues for the parent and child to understand the reasons why the child responds in the way they do.

The less our comments seem like questions the easier it will be to create the right conditions for your child to respond comfortably. It's even possible to ask questions without them seeming like questions!

- Is the goal still relevant?

- Could you run over the main points again? I want to get them totally clear in my mind.

- From your remarks, I understand Mr Smith agreed to look at your work again. Can you tell me what has happened since then?

Case Study: The Knaq

We need to understand the power of good questions. How about we take some of the above information into a practical example, right now? Coach Laura Berman Fortgang[2] has a term she calls Wisdom Accessing Questions. In this approach she generally avoids 'Why' and mostly targets 'What', to commence questions.

The case study below covers the same topic between Mother and child, with very different results. In the first, you'll hear a more conventional approach. The second approach uses what we like to call 'Knowledge Accessing Questions – easy to remember as the Knaq (knack!)

Sam: I'm not happy about this situation and I don't know why.

Mum: Why do you think that is?

Sam: No idea. I keep thinking about it, but it's very confusing.

Mum: Why do you think its bothering you?

Sam: It's something about 'Sir'....

Mum: Was it something he said to you?

Sam: Oh, he said he knew someone who could help me with my maths and then when I asked who, he wouldn't tell me.

Mum: How did that make you feel?

Sam: Angry.

Mum: Did any one thing annoy you?

Sam: No – it was everything!

---

[2] Refer to Recommended Reading

Mum: Do you know what you want to do now?

Sam: Just drop it, I think. But I'm just not sure.

The parent's questions focus on information seeking. They are not specific, so Sam is not being specific either. The result is no progress and further frustration.

Compare that approach with the example below, where the parent coach (Mum) uses the Knaq approach.

Sam: I'm not happy about this situation and I don't know why.

Mum: Take a guess – what is it that's bugging you?

Sam: I don't know.

Mum: If you did know, *what* would you say?

Sam: Probably I don't trust 'Sir'.

Mum: You don't trust 'Sir'. *What* made you decide that?

Sam: He has been very vague. He won't commit to anything he has said. I've even asked him about it.

Mum: What do you need to move ahead?

Sam: I need to find someone I can trust.

Mum: Great. Any ideas who could help?

Sam: Yes. There's another teacher I think could give me an idea.

Mum: When will you call him?

Sam: Today!

Fantastic. Here Sam gets immediate clarity and because action is taken, tension relief as well. This is simply the result of using a Knaq approach.

A key distinction about using the Knaq question structure is to direct attention away from details and explanations, and towards outcomes (i.e.

Goals). It's too easy to get drawn into trying to understand what's happening. It's far more powerful to move toward becoming a collaborator with your child in developing solutions. You'll also discover it's far less stressful on you the parent, as you no longer have to 'be an expert'! In summary – you are aiming to establish exactness or specifics in the answers elicited from your questions.

LISTENING

If we improve our questioning skills we must certainly make sure we don't miss the answers! *The Coaching Parent* is dependent upon enhanced listening skills. In our coaching relationships as we build trust, emotional content can also increase. Similarly when the person is important to us, we want to be confident we are listening and responding appropriately. The more attention we pay when someone is talking, the more attention they will pay when it's our turn.

One of the biggest barriers to communication is an inability to listen. Listening ought to be easy, yet it is actually very difficult, as there are many barriers to effective listening other than the desire to reply or interrupt.

Small wonder then that mastering inter–personal communication is challenging.

Whatever the purpose of our communication, at its best it involves active listening, honest expression of thought and emotions and change in our relationships. This is worth emphasising – *Change in our relationships*. Without the possibility of change, the communication process is sterile, lifeless and without meaning.

When you tell me something I did not know about you, it may change how I perceive you, how I feel about you or how I conduct myself around you. The same goes for me too. We are now relating to each other differently, although the difference may be subtle. This is true then when interacting with our children.

One of the key components in this change is active listening.

What Is Active Listening?

Active listening certainly involves use of critical thinking skills, such as recalling related issues, questioning, agreeing, disagreeing, and reaching logical conclusions. But its primary purpose is: *to understand the meaning of the message from the speaker's point of view.* Whenever you listen actively to another person's comments, your reason for doing so is to understand. Your aim is to enter as much as possible into the world of the person who is speaking; to listen with your heart and gut as well as with your ears and brain.

To listen actively means that while you're taking in what's being said, you're not busy evaluating, judging, blaming, labeling, interpreting, thinking about how you're going to respond, speculating about where the conversation is likely to lead or considering whether you appear to be paying attention while your mind is drifting to the next telephone call you need to make. Instead, you are focused entirely on using the verbal and nonverbal clues you're receiving to understand and appreciate where this person is coming from, how he feels about what he is saying, why he feels that way, and what the meaning of his words are to him and *his life*. So how do you know if you're listening actively?

SOME USEFUL LISTENING TECHNIQUES

Reflective Listening

This is a technique that should be used if:

- The message you are receiving is very complex.

- It is important that you retain some or all of the information.

It is a method of understanding by putting the speaker's words into your own words. There are two methods of doing this:

Summary Questions

You should use these to immediately clarify something of which you're unsure. They are often phrased as:

'As I understand it ... Is that right?'

or

'So what you are saying is ... Is that what you mean?'

For example: *"Let's see if I've got this right. You want to switch courses at college, but you're worried about how your tutor will react. You think the college will let you do Italian – but it depends on your results – have I got that right?"*

Using summary questions prevents any misunderstandings that may arise from continuing.

Reflective Statements

How can you tell if what you think someone means is really what they mean? Most people simply assume they know. They hear someone say something, and then they quickly consider what it might mean and select what they believe to be the most likely interpretation. When you're an active listener, you go farther than that. You check to make sure, rather than presuming you know what is meant. This kind of assumption checking is known as "reflective" listening, because it reflects back to the speaker your best guess about the meaning that you've heard. It asks for confirmation, denial, or adjustment if necessary. It can be delivered either in the form of a question or as a simple statement.

When you listen actively, you're also listening empathetically, and the message you send by doing so is critically important. You're saying, *"I think I've heard you correctly and I'm also working hard to understand how you might feel."* This is a message that builds trust and enables greater openness and equality of relationship. It also gives the child a chance to hear him/herself think, to "live in the question" for a moment and see what other thoughts, feelings, and responses emerge, before you jump in with a response, a change of conversational direction, or a prescription to try and fix things.

ACTIVE LISTENING – KEY ASPECTS

Here are some things you can do to become a world–class active listener, in support of your journey to becoming *The Coaching Parent.* They are not difficult, but, as with any new behaviour, it will take some practice before they begin to feel like second nature. You'll need to work on all these things constantly to hone your coaching skills.

1. Make a sincere commitment to become an active listener.

Bring your desire to listen more effectively into your consciousness several times a day. Remind yourself why you want to acquire or sharpen this skill and what it will do for you and those you care about when you've mastered it. When someone else is talking, listen closely and actively at all times. It enriches both of us when I understand what is going on inside the speaker, as well as the content of the message being sent.

2. Take a few moments to prepare yourself to listen.

Eliminate distractions and potential distractions. Put away your mental clutter, too. Remove your preoccupations, worries, or daydreams to a set of mental parentheses. You can easily retrieve them later. Focus your complete attention on the communication that is taking place, no matter how long or short it is likely to be.

3. Wait patiently until your child is finished speaking.

Don't interrupt. Your first task is to be certain you understand what has been said and how the other person feels about it. If you're not sure you understand then try a statement or question that seeks more information, such as, *"Would you tell me more about that?"*, rather than trying to clarify or interpret what you've heard. Jumping to conclusions too quickly or being too eager to arrive at a solution can lead to difficulties down the line when you realise you didn't have the complete picture.

4. Place your analytical skills on reserve.

Don't mentally linger over one idea even though the speaker has gone on to another. Keep up with the flow of information, unless you're beginning to feel lost and need clarification. Avoid shifting your focus to yourself in order to plan how you'll respond when it's your turn to talk. Your intention as an active, empathetic coach is to understand, not to critique, analyse, advise, or argue. After you're certain you fully understand, you may, or may not, choose to look more critically and logically at message content.

5. Notice nonverbal clues.

This is the benefit in our face–to face interactions. We already know that not all communication comes to us through language and that most of the messages we send one another are in the form of nonverbal signals (body language). Posture, gestures, tone of voice, sighs, muscle tension, and facial expressions often convey more to an observant listener than what is actually being said. Pay attention to these important signals, and learn to read them. See *Chapter 5: Rapport* and in particular Card 3.

6. Check your assumptions to make sure you have understood.

Reflect back to your child your understanding of the full message conveyed. *"You're really excited about getting into the team, although I sense you have some concerns."* Wait for confirmation or correction, and indicate when you have understood. *"Okay, I think I understand what you mean now."*, *"I see. It's not that you're reluctant to talk with me. You're actually worried about letting someone else down."*

7. Think of listening based on the ratio of having two ears and one mouth.

Use them in that ratio. Listen twice as much as you speak.

8. Maintain eye contact.

Remember that in some cultures total eye contact is unacceptable. In Japan, listeners are taught to focus on a speaker's neck in order to avoid eye contact, while in the U.S., listeners are encouraged to gaze into a speaker's eyes.

Some individuals including adults find that "unnecessary tension" is created by eye contact, or lack of it. If this applies to you then perhaps your belief system (usually irrational beliefs) is causing your tension, annoyance, and/or other emotional issues. Some of your irrational beliefs might be that others won't respond to you unless you have direct eye contact, or that you're not good at socialising, and never will be because you can't maintain eye contact.

Rather than focus on the other person, think of what you'd like to know about them and ask. Smile. Compliment her. Pay attention to what she tells you. This changes your focus from you to her, and will help alleviate some of your stress and anxiety.

Accept your inability to initiate or maintain eye contact, keep it from becoming worse, and actively try to change it for the better.

The benefits are considerable. It shows your child that you are paying attention. Also a direct gaze without staring or holding eye contact too long (along with forward body and smiling) is usually a reliable indicator of good feeling.

You might be thinking, "How long is too long for eye contact?" The answer is once you feel uncomfortable or you notice your child is uncomfortable. You'll soon establish these implicit rules between you both.

9. Allow others to finish their own sentences.

No matter how enthusiastically you want to jump into the conversation – hold back. Doing so will indicate respect for what the person is saying.

10. Get all the information that is available within a conversation.

You do not want to jump to any false conclusions. Wait for the end of the sentence or end of the conversation to be sure this conversation is unique from any other that may sound similar to you.

11. Respond so the other person knows you are listening.

Your response may be *"Yes"* or *"I see"* or merely nodding your head. Any of these will do.

OBSTACLES TO LISTENING

There are so many ways to respond to something you've just heard; yet responding isn't the same as listening. Here is a list of those responses known to interrupt the listening process – you may be able to identify others:

1. Giving advice, making suggestions, or providing solutions

2. Persuading with logic, arguing, or lecturing

3. Moralising, preaching, or telling someone what they "should" do

4. Disagreeing, judging, criticising, or blaming

5. Agreeing, approving, or praising

6. Interpreting or analysing, distorting what's being said

7. Thinking of other things/lack of interest

8. Reassuring, sympathising, or consoling

9. Questioning or probing

10. Withdrawing, distracting, humoring, or changing the subject

11. Assuming that you won't understand

12. Being distracted by emotive words/jargon

13. Outside distractions

14. Not valuing the person being listened to

This isn't to say these responses should never be used, but within your conversation, there is a proper time and place for them. It's important to realise that while you're responding in ways that seem helpful and positive – for example supporting, praising, approving, sympathising, proposing or reassuring – you're not actively listening. You may just miss something more significant.

Much can be gleaned from *active observation* as well as active listening. People often reveal their feelings in the way they look and in their body language. Most children have still to learn about how or why to discuss these activities, reinforcing the importance of observation. Feelings go into the heart of the person and if you show you have tuned into those feelings then you show a high degree of empathy – the key to strong relationships and an enhanced parent/child understanding.

Decide to listen actively, more carefully and responsively from now on. Listen and acknowledge what you hear, even if you don't agree with it, before expressing your experience or point of view.

Finally, remember to maintain a balance that's just right for you and your child of using your Head and Heart. See Card 35 in *Chapter 9: Optimising Stress.*

Exercise One

Questioning and Listening

Now that you perhaps know a little more about questioning and listening, what key things have you noticed?

1. _____

_____

2. _____

_____

3. _____

_____

4. _____

_____

Self–Coaching

What will you do differently next time you are having a conversation with your child?

1. _____

_____

2. _____

_____

3. _____

_____

4. _____

_____

CHAPTER FOUR

GROW Your Kids!

You now know a key aspect of coaching is about raising awareness and responsibility. Your intention with your child is for them to become empowered to do what until now, they might have believed impossible. In effect, they will want to take charge of their own destiny.

It starts by asking the right kind of questions…

We suggest a 'model' or way of coaching referred to as the 'GROW' model. It will require practice to enable you to use it flawlessly. Even then, after many conversations, you will be aware of things you might have said differently. Don't worry though as the aim is to practice enough so that it becomes a habit and feels natural.

GROW was championed by Sir John Whitmore in his book Coaching for Performance[3]. We offer it as an easy to use and well–established coaching model. There are numerous alternatives including SCORE, LASER, 5QF, 'Succeed' et al. We believe GROW forms an excellent 'starter' to enable anyone to easily use, and rapidly master, a structure for coaching. It does not necessarily need to be used step by step and we have found that checking current situation (*Reality* in the model) is often a great starting point because it addresses the question, "How do you know that you need to change anything?" The more knowledgeable coach will already appreciate and integrate other good models too.

Have in mind your overriding parenting intention:

---

[3] Refer Recommended Reading

"What's the best way I can help you to learn how to deal with this [the challenge or problem they bring to you] yourself?"

If the above question is *your* Goal then how can you find out the goal of your child? The diagram below will assist you in understanding the approach.

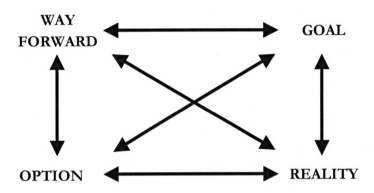

Look at the above diagram and consider the following questions about your child:

What is their **Goal**? What do they want?

What is the **Reality** now? What's happening and is there anything missing?

What **Options** do they have to get the goal?

What are they committed to doing? What is the **Way Forward**?

We will go into all of these headings in detail in just a moment. Before doing that though let's make a key point. Its usually best to start first with the **Goal,** then be flexible by going around the above model in *any order* that works. Don't get stuck on one section and that *includes* the Goal – be patient, move on and then return to get more detail later. This requires practice and a little faith that what you are doing will work. Trust us – it does! Leave the **Way Forward** to the very end – the reason for this is explained shortly. Help your child to be clear on what you are discussing – a first step on the road to achieving success. Some coaching models call this the 'Topic' or 'Subject'. Keep it simple by checking your shared understanding. For example say: "Are we talking here about your homework marks or a lack of time to do it to the standard that's needed?" Remember before you can help your child to establish a goal, they must have an issue, topic, challenge, subject, problem, etc to work on. Make the language fit the situation. Clarity here will serve both of you well once you start discussing the Goal. Don't be frightened to revisit to refine the exact topic as it becomes clearer through the conversation.

GOAL

"A dream with an action plan attached to it"

The power of goals is incredible. All our success is based on deciding on what we want to have or achieve, and creating a goal in our minds to allow us to get it.

Some time ago a survey carried out in one of America's top universities was commissioned to find what determined long–term student career success. The survey found that only 3% of students had written their goals down before the end of their final year. 20 years after graduation, the goal setters who wrote their goals down had accumulated as much **total** wealth as the other 97% who hadn't **combined**!

The above story, told for many years, is powerful and compelling! Sadly it's now widely believed to be purely anecdotal.

However I [David] have noticed the success difference between mental and written goals. I've lost count of how often I review results and am amazed to note what's actually happened. I was scanning an old learning journal where I had documented our business goals for the next three years. Upon inspection most of them were achieved within 18 months. I was totally amazed. This has also happened many times with clients.

Depending on the language skills and understanding levels of your child, pay attention to the 'Goal word'. Some youngsters are more responsive to "What do you want to achieve" or "what's your aim here" rather than insisting they respond to your demand for a 'Goal'. So relax and remember your intention and resulting language are the keys in this communication. For more resources see *Chapter 5: Rapport*.

The key point we are making about goals, is their power is *amplified* by the two stages of first considering them carefully and then committing them to paper. Don't fall into the trap of saying, "I know my goals", without also writing them down and regularly reviewing them.

When you know what they and you want to talk about, find out what they want to achieve or change. Ask them:

1. Imagine your situation in the future, as you want it to be, and describe it to me.

Get them to live the goal, by asking them to see it, hear it and feel it. The power of our imagination is amazing and experiencing in advance, what it's like to achieve a goal, is very motivating for most of us.

And later, when they are totally committed to it, after sharpening it up with REALITY, OPTIONS and THE WAY FORWARD, ask:

2. What are you experiencing – seeing, hearing, feeling, maybe even smelling and tasting – that tells you the goal has been achieved?

So, when you have the Goal described, check out your child's Reality…

REALITY

What is *reality*? What is real to you is not real to someone else. It is your child's reality that matters here, not yours. No two people ever experience the world in the same way, not even identical twins!

Remember – Your intention with your child is for them to become empowered to do what, until then, they might have believed impossible.

As with all talks with your child, *listen* to them. They have the answers within; your goal is to find the best way to help them learn how to get their goal themselves. Work hard to resist being their advisor.

So, to confirm where they are now (their Reality) ask:

1. What is happening now that tells you there is an issue, challenge, or opportunity?

And then:

2. As well as what is happening – what is missing from your Reality that you would like to have?

So you now have found out what they want (the **Goal**), and where they are now 'in their world' (**Reality**). The next step is to help them create **Options** to close the gap…

OPTIONS

Let's be honest, most of us know in our hearts that there is always more than one way of doing things.

Children have vivid imaginations, the more vivid the better, so let's say part of them is creative, and loves being challenged to come up with a few ways to get the goal. In looking for the best way to help them, they will find and then choose the best **Option** for themselves.

Think back to a feeling of being stuck. Another way of saying this is that there is no single best way, or only one unappealing way out of the situation.

So, to get their creative part working, ask:

1. Describe and ideally write down at least SIX things you could do. Don't think — just write. Assume anything is possible.

If you have a particular time constraint, leave out the writing down, and work with at least two of the six options, simply so that choice exists — this is important. Now you want them to commit to their chosen **Option** (having begun to create a new **Reality)** that will get their **Goal**, so what is the **Way Forward?**

WAY FORWARD

Taking action without insight can lead to trouble, yet without action nothing ever happens.

Your coaching is leading your child to a position where they are no longer stuck, and are moving towards their prized goal. This coaching session ends when they are 100% committed to the actions they will take to get their goal.

Quite often, as we've already said, you will need to move around the **GROW** model before the goal becomes really clear.

So, now they have the **Goal**, they know what is happening now, and what might be missing, which will secure their goal. They have created some **Options**. Ask them:

1. Which option appeals most?

You don't need them to explain their reasons, although they usually will — what's important is that *they* know why and are motivated to take action.

2. What will you do and when? List the actions you must go through to complete this thing that you have chosen.

This question will allow them to choose their favoured option. If they are not committed to any option they have created, asking them to imagine or sense doing it will lead to its rejection in favour of the one they truly want to do.

Where next? Back to the second question under **Goal**:

2. What are you experiencing, i.e. seeing, hearing, feeling, maybe even smelling or tasting, that tells you the goal has been achieved?

Once you have this, and pay great attention to their body language, voice tone and overall 'state', fix a time to re–visit and review what they are about to do. Make this timescale realistic, no more than two weeks, ideally one.

In the meantime, if they bring another issue, challenge, or opportunity to you, start again by finding out their **Goal.**

If they are not committed to this course of action, re–visit the **Options, Reality** and **Goal** again.

The following diagram is a brief summary of the basic questions for each subject area of the model. Add some of those mentioned above to enlarge your learning. If you feel encouraged to read further about GROW, you will find some advocates who offer dozens of different questions to ask in each area. Should that appeal to you, we would say experiment and find what works best. Keep in mind that you won't ever be failing, just finding other ways to become an even better Coaching Parent.

Goal	Reality
• Imagine your situation in the future, and as you want it to be – describe it.	• What is happening now that tells you there is an issue, challenge, or opportunity?
• What are you experiencing that tells you the goal has been achieved?	• As well as what is happening – what is missing from your Reality that you would like to have?
• What are others doing that tells you that you have succeeded?	• How does what you have achieved compare with what you hoped for?
• When do you want to be in this position – the one that you can see in your mind's eye? (You must have a time–scale in mind. Next week? Next month? Next year? It must be realistic.)	• What obstacles are in your way that prevent or hinder you from moving forward?

Options	Way Forward
• Describe and ideally write down SIX things you could do. Don't think, just write. Assume anything is possible.	• What will you do and when? List the actions you must go through to complete this thing that you have chosen.
• What could you do if you didn't have to explain it or be answerable to anyone?	• Should anyone else be involved in this list of things you are going to do to complete, this thing that you have chosen?
• What could you do if time were unlimited?	• When will you tell them?

WELL DONE!

You have found the best way to help your child to learn how to meet challenges or solve problems themselves!

We can never give or receive enough praise. Praise of course which comes from the heart and has no hidden agenda or other motive.

WHAT IS YOUR WAY FORWARD?

Well, let's assume your Goal is to help your child *realise their dreams*, and to do so might involve working smarter or harder at school, or becoming more committed to a sport, hobby or spare time activity.

Your Reality may be that your child is coming home upset or angry. Or maybe they have discovered a talent for singing, or acting, or fixing cars. They may even have a chance to go to university…

And if they're angry or withdrawn, you may have found out they want to stop being bullied. If upset, they may have fallen out with a mate, or have been ignored by a teacher. They may have no idea how to develop their talents, or believe they could go to and succeed at university.

Their Options, which you help them create, may include reporting the bully, facing up to them, or taking martial arts classes; inviting their friend for tea, inviting new friends for tea, showing more enthusiasm at school, believing in themselves; doing part–time work, taking lessons, watching learning videos, reading, talking to experts; running through what a university education would be like, helping plan a career path…

And their Way Forward is to consider the options, run through in their mind what it will be like to take them, and choose the one that their heart knows is the best…

When the moment arises, you might realise they would benefit from an ever–deepening level of self–confidence. In helping or wanting to influence anyone, this can only be done, without resorting to harmful threats, by getting into rapport. Most of us could use ways to make learning more enjoyable easier and faster. And lastly, what about using 'stress' to our advantage?

Exercise Two

GROW Your Kids!

Now that you have read about this coaching model, what have you discovered?

1. _____

_____

2. _____

_____

3. _____

_____

4. _____

_____

Self–Coaching

What will you do differently as a result of this knowledge?

1. _____

_____

2. _____

_____

3. _____

_____

4. _____

_____

CHAPTER FIVE

Rapport

**"If you get along really well with someone,
the two of you have rapport."**

The purpose of this chapter is:

- To improve the rapport between you and your child.

- To develop your and your child's influencing and rapport skills.

This chapter is written as if a child is speaking to you so it will help if you put yourself into the shoes and maybe the ears of the listener!

PROMPT CARDS

This is the first chapter in which we introduce the idea of prompt or learning cards. One approach we've found works is to ask your child to read the card and then discuss it with them. Another is for you to read the chapter and then decide which cards serve both of you best.

Alongside the cards there are several questions. Normal text is for you to consider. Where a question is in italics, we suggest exploring it with your child.

TRUST

Any coaching demands a high level of trust.

If trust is in need of attention, you have several options for gaining and building on trust:

- *What can I do so that you trust me more?*

- *How can we rebuild trust?*

- *Could you convince someone else <u>you</u> are trustworthy – how?*

- *How can I help you trust Mr/Ms X more?*

Trust in specific areas:

- *What do I do that you're not sure about?*

- *I'm new to this, so could you give me time to develop your trust in me?*

As a way of monitoring progress continuously ask your child and yourself:

- *How are we/am I doing?*

The messages on the card that follows are a reminder of both the fragile nature and power of trust.

TRUST

Can I trust you?

If I can, I will be open with you, I will
feel safe, and I will be honest.

If I can't, I will be guarded, feel anxious, and may not be honest.

Trust is a feeling, one that I can't always explain.

I may trust you with one thing, but not with
another. It's nothing personal.

Trust has limits; without them, we may both be at risk.

Trust may take years to develop, a minute to lose.

Trust is wonderful, it helps me grow, deepens my respect for you.
It makes our relationship a source of joy, learning, and support.
The more you trust me, the less control I feel. The less control I
feel, the more responsibility I take.

You look trustworthy, you sound trustworthy,
just let me check my feelings...

RESPECT

Respect and trust are different. Respect is about placing a higher value on a person or relationship. You may trust someone, but pay little attention to him or her.

You may respect someone, possibly for who they are, and/or their achievements, but not trust them.

How do you respect <u>yourself</u>?

The coaching parent must respect their child. Respecting your child means respecting them as a person, but not necessarily their behaviour. It is about listening to their opinions, loving them despite your differences, and understanding how they learn and get along in the world. It is about giving them time. Card 2 brings these into sharp focus.

Questions to ask to help nurture respect:

- *When we disagree, what do we do to get back/maintain respect?*

- *How might I respect you <u>even more</u>?*

- *How might you respect yourself <u>even more</u>?*

RESPECT

2

Do you care [value] what I think?

Sometimes we don't agree. If you don't respect me, I've nothing to lose. If you do, it makes it easier for me to respect myself, and to respect you.

When I'm angry, I don't always want to talk. Sometimes, give me time to cool down.

If I do speak, please don't interrupt me or tell me what you think. Ask me about it, it's hard for me to tell you, so make it easier.

I like it when you encourage me to be open, because it builds up if I keep it to myself.

I like it when you want to know how I feel, and you let me know how you are thinking, and want to work it out with me.

And you respect me when you realise I'm not broke and don't need fixing.

You respect me when you find out how I learn, help me become aware of it, and act on it.

I respect you, when you respect yourself.

BODY LANGUAGE

The major part of rapport is how you are, more than what you say or how you say it. This reveals itself all too obviously in how we hold ourselves and move! Before covering the specifics, share these questions:

- *How do you know you are in rapport with someone?*

- *What do you do to get rapport?*

- *How do you maintain rapport?*

- *If you lose rapport, how do you get it back?*

Card 3 describes 'matching' and 'mis–matching' behaviours. Matching your child's posture and gestures will enable you to positively influence them. This must be handled with care though as it can be over done and look like mockery! Avoid any attempt to manipulate, as you will eventually be found out.

The way our eyes move give clues as to whether we are remembering pictures or sounds or talking to ourselves, or whether we are creating pictures or sounds, or going into our feelings[4]. This will happen even if we are trying to maintain eye contact.

---

[4] Check out this in any basic book on NLP (Neuro–Linguistic Programming). One of the best is 'Way of NLP' by Joseph O'Connor and Ian Mc Dermott, pub Thorsons, 2001.

BODY LANGUAGE

3

Should I do as you do, or as you say?

I don't know why, but I don't believe you when you
tell me you love me, and look at the ceiling.

Sometimes, we argue, but I still feel welcome and supported.

I notice that when you sit or stand like me, we get on.

I notice, even when you agree with me, if you turn
away, or sit or stand different from me, we fall out.

I've even noticed when we look like bookends,
because it feels good.

I feel the real me when you look,
sound and move like me... Magic!

An estimate of the effectiveness of face–to–face communication[5] suggests that in any message 7% of the impact is contained in our words, 35% in the tone we use, and the remaining 58% in our non–spoken (sometimes called body language) gestures.

Of course, *certain* words have massive impact, and we are often not aware of our tonality and body language. Perhaps this is the time to become more aware?

Try out the following with a friend first, then your child, just for a minute or two. It will help you understand the importance of body language:

- *Agree with each other verbally, and 'mismatch' non–verbally.*

- *Disagree with each other verbally, and match each other non–verbally.*

- *What gives us the greater rapport?*

- *How can you use what you have just learned?*

- *How and when are you going to apply the learning?*

After reading the next two cards, try these questions:

- *When people are in rapport, what do you Notice? Hear? Feel?*

- *What internal pictures/images, or sounds, or feelings do you experience when in rapport?*

If you don't like someone, yet still want or need rapport, what do you do? Well, depending on how important the relationship is – act as if you *do* like them. 'Positive regard' works wonders.

---

[5] These figures are based on considerable research. They may vary depending on circumstance, and make the point strongly...

THE POWER OF WORDS

While body language may be all powerful, rapport can still be broken with one ill chosen word.

Words have a big impact. The nature of the impact will depend on the energy behind the words, in the form of tonality and body language, and also the intention. In nurturing and communicating with our children, our words are hugely significant.

The first five questions on Card 4 show how messages can be directed towards the behaviour or the person. Behaviour can be changed; it is difficult to change *who we are*!

Ever heard of the child who grew up thinking his name was No?[6]

---

[6] We can't give you the exact reference, but there must be thousands of poor souls so condemned. Dave Pelzer has written a trilogy of books starting with 'A Child Called It' [published by Orion] Get it if you want to read the inspirational story of how he overcame probably the worst example of parenting ever told.

A WORD PAINTS A THOUSAND PICTURES

Stupid! ... Do I resemble that remark?

Is what *I'm doing* stupid, or am *I* stupid?

Is what *I'm doing* hopeless, or am *I* hopeless?

Is what *I'm doing* brilliant, or am *I* brilliant?

Is what *I'm doing* sound, and am *I* sound?

Sticks and stones may break my bones,
and words can shape me...

I like praise for what *I do*, and I like
praise for who *I am* even more.

If I'm wrong, tell me what *I'm doing* wrong,
and leave the real me alone.

The real me does what's right for me, so help
me know if what I'm doing isn't right for others.

Tell me what to do, avoid telling me what not to do!

Don't think of the remarks you resembled when you were young!

Help your child to develop awareness of their inner world:

- *What image or picture does the word 'No' create in your mind? And 'Yes'?*
- *Where in the body are the feelings you get when hearing the word 'Yes'? No?*
- *How could I give you 'bad news' in ways that educate, rather than deflate?*

Many of us struggle to respond positively to phrases like: "Don't do X, don't do Y". Our mind automatically deletes the word "don't."

Don't think of green snow…

As a little challenge can you re–phrase the sentence; *"Thank you for not smoking"* remaining courteous, and avoiding any use of the word 'no'? Try this with your child[7]

Please think before putting an emotional charge in your message, especially if it's negative. Most of us are not aware that we are doing it. Use the questions below to find and then change the emotional impact of your voice tone.

For you and your child:

- *How do you know what emotion (love, criticism, feedback, praise or blame) there is in someone's voice?*
- *How do you know what emotion (love, criticism, feedback, praise or blame) there is in my voice?*
- *What might increase your capacity to know?*
- *How might we ensure the right emotion is communicated?*

Experiment with changing negative emotional language to positive, and again get feedback to confirm it.

---

[7] Isn't it difficult to stop someone having moved from a 'normal' state? Telling people to stop smoking/drinking/taking drugs almost inevitably begs a negative. How about 'thank you for breathing clean air'?

IT AIN'T WHAT YOU SAY, IT'S THE WAY THAT YOU SAY IT

5

I AM NOT SHOUTING!

If I hear love in your voice, I'll listen because I feel valued.

If I hear criticism, I might listen, but we'll
both go down in each other's estimation.

Feedback can sound like criticism,
criticism can sound like feedback.

You can make praise seem like blame,
and blame seem like praise.

You can choose your tone, just as much as your words.

A moment's thought, gets the right words, the right
tone, and the right pose to deliver them.

Watch or listen to me to confirm it.

VALUES

The kinds of things we value determine our behaviour. In valuing someone we respect them. Self–evidently, what we value – what is important to us – gets more of our time and energy.

Card 6 is about how our children copy *what we value.*

The word *congruence* describes the match or fit between an individual's inner feelings and outer display[8].

Carl Rogers, arguably the most influential psychologist in American history, found that congruence of feelings and actions can never be total, but his experience convinced him that choosing to be real with others is vital. "In my relationship with persons, I've found that it does not help, in the long run, to act as though I was something I was not."

By sending out mixed messages, your child will probably pick *actions* to copy, rather than words.

- *What kind of things do you value?*

- *How might I discover them without asking?*

- *What kind of things do you think I value?*

- *How did you come to appreciate X?*

- *What would have to happen for you to appreciate Y?*

If we do not honour what we value and we lack congruence, then we will struggle to gain true rapport with others. In effect, we will not be authentic. Valuing ourselves is critical. If we neglect our health, our needs for rest or our loved ones, then we are sending out the message, "I and you don't count."

---

[8] Carl Rogers, "This Is Me," in *On Becoming a Person*, Houghton Mifflin, Boston, 1961, p. 24.

VALUES

Who are you?

What is really important to you? I think you care about other people, and don't like lies. I'm not sure about other things. I often wonder if you want me to value what you think is important.

Of course you know if I think you value:

- Love, I value love.
- Criticism, I value criticism.
- Feedback, I value feedback.

When you're not around, if I see/read/hear about killing and violence being right, about war being just and or about one skin colour being better than another, I may believe it.

If I watch violence, brutality and corruption, I may value them.

I value what you value, unless what you say matters is the opposite of what you do.

If you value yourself, I may begin to value myself...

CONGRUENCE

What can you do to love and accept *yourself* unconditionally, like you do your child?

The congruent person is genuine, real, integrated, whole and transparent.

The non–congruent person tries to impress, plays a role, puts up a front, and hides behind a façade.

Maybe congruence requires practice?

What does the way you walk and move reveal or say about you?

The message of Card 7 is... begin to help yourself and your child become more aware of the times you 'walk one way', and talk another:

- *How do people decide what to pay attention to when watching or listening to others?*

- *What do you notice in other people when making a judgement about them?*

- *How can we both ensure we walk our talk?*

What value would you place on hypocrisy?

WALKING MY TALK

Do you really believe that?

I watch what you do, listen to what you say,
and sometimes it feels good.

I watch what you do, listen to what you say,
and sometimes it feels strange.

I wonder sometimes when you say
'I love this' that you might hate it...

I watch my heroes and they look as if they love what they're
doing, say they love it, and it feels to me that they do.

How can I hide my true feelings, so as not to upset you?

Is life about filling it full of what you have to hide your feelings
about; or is it about finding what you love, removing
any obstacles and then doing it?

Please do as you say, even though I might not like all of it.

PACING & LEADING

Traditional wisdom tells us that when someone is angry or upset, we should remain calm and *talk* them out if it. This may not always be a successful technique.

Card 8 borrows the principles of copying behaviour. As adults, we can exert our influence powerfully and productively by matching (*pacing*) our children if we want to help them out of negative states (*leading*).

Beware trying to 'fix' them though!

The following card gives examples of how you can learn this. Before teaching your child, find out if they naturally use this approach anyway:

- *If your friend/ sister/ brother gets angry, what do you do?*

- *When is it best not to interfere?*

- *What do you see or feel that tells you they would like to let go of the anger?*

- *How about if you got angry like them, then helped them become calm?*

- *How can this approach be used to help them learn more?*

When helping your child with homework, or to solve a problem, what happens if you ever become confused?

If you match the other person's breathing, how much stronger might your rapport become? Try it…

PACING & LEADING

I can now look back and laugh...

How can I learn when you are so far ahead of me?

How can you learn when I'm ahead of you?

When I'm angry, match my anger [become angry like me], then lead me to calm from anger. Move from anger by first becoming frustrated [then I will become frustrated rather than angry] and then becoming irritated [then I will become irritated rather than frustrated], and finally by becoming calm – when you become calm, I will too.

When I'm upset, match my upset state [become upset like me], then lead me to being OK from upset. Move from upset by first becoming sad [then I will become sad rather than upset] and then becoming disappointed [then I will become disappointed rather than sad], and finally by being OK – when you become OK, I will too.

When I'm stuck lead me to learning through confusion, curiosity and understanding. Become stuck, then move from stuck to confused, then confused to curious, and then from being curious to understanding. And finally from understanding to learning!

Become me for a short while, and then let me follow you, as you become you again...

SPACE

Why should it matter where we stand or sit in relation to others?

It matters because you may be breaking rapport.

To find out where both your best and worst places are, take turns to sit in the middle of a room with space all around you. Ask your child to walk slowly around you through 360°, about a few feet way. Ask them to stop when you feel different.

Are there any places you feel uncomfortable? More comfortable? Is it possible these places may change, or be different in different rooms?

How can you influence your teacher to become more aware of your space?

In Closing…

A few more general rapport questions:

Is it me you like, or what I do?

If you don't like someone, yet still want or need rapport, what do you do?

What single thing, were you to do it, would improve the rapport you had with yourself?

Knowing there is far more to rapport than we have covered in here, how can you learn even more?

MY SPACE

9

Don't stand so close to me...

Some days, I want you to respect my space,
and keep your distance.

Other days, come as close as you normally do.

There are places, especially behind me, when you are
in them, which make me feel uncomfortable.

There are places in front or at the side of me,
which block my thinking and learning.

There are places, on days or times when it matters,
when I can show you exactly where to sit or stand.

There are sounds or noises that invade my personal space.

My favourite places and spaces help me learn, relax and grow.

Exercise Three

Rapport

There is a lot to rapport isn't there? Has that surprised you or did you already have this appreciation – if you did learn something useful, what was it?

1. _____

_____

2. _____

_____

3. _____

_____

4. _____

_____

Self–Coaching

Where will you focus most of your rapport attention in the future?

1. _____

_____

2. _____

_____

3. _____

_____

4. _____

_____

CHAPTER SIX

Self-Confidence

**"...I've believed as many as six impossible
things before breakfast"**

Through The Looking Glass, by Lewis Carroll

As parents we know that self-confidence is vital if we are to achieve anything. It's a wide subject with many aspects including:

- Self-esteem

- Self-worth

- Self-image

- Self-believe

- Self-respect

- Realising potential

SELF–ESTEEM

While this whole chapter is about self–confidence, self–esteem is often spoken of in the same breath to mean confidence.

"Our Thomas has low self–esteem," "If only Emily had higher self–esteem." etc.

In this chapter we need to bear in mind that many of the titles may seem to describe something similar, far more than in any other of the chapters. That's because *they do* – each part of our sense of identity is tightly integrated into the whole subject. It's not something many of us tend to fully consider. However it's worth attempting to break the overall topic down into manageable chunks for when you work with your child.

Read Card 10 on the next page.

Consider the 1st paragraph.

You'll note it starts negatively. A little later on in card 13 we explain this in greater detail – unfortunately for the average person most inner dialogue, or self–talk as it's sometimes called, is negative. How does this relate to you?

What might happen if you discuss this 1st paragraph with your child?

Consider the 3rd paragraph. Ask your child these questions:

- *Which clothes do you prefer to wear that make you feel confident?*

- *What do you think might be the reason?*

Now to enhance your child's and your own learning…

- *In which clothes do you feel less confident?*

What additional questions can you come up with?

SELF-ESTEEM
[CONFIDENCE]

How good?

If I don't feel good about myself or confident in my own ability to do things or to learn then I won't master anything. I will find learning a pain. I will close myself down, take no risks, avoid people and imagine dark things about my appearance.
High self-esteem helps me excel.

Self-esteem can vary in an instant. We can begin learning a task, and feel good as we make progress. Then, when we hit a problem, or lack understanding of what we are facing, for that moment, our self-esteem can drop.

We can [temporarily] boost our self-esteem by good clothes, a good meal or mastering a task.

Our self-esteem can be lowered by a series of setbacks, or by people constantly telling, or implying, we're not good enough.

Self-esteem grows over time when we become more responsible for our lives, take [realistic] risks, heal our past, let go of grudges and resentment. 'Mistakes' are how we learn and grow.
We often need help to do these things.

Mastery flows when we feel we deserve success.

SELF–WORTH

Have you ever said or thought, "I'm not worthy of this?"

This is a statement of your self–worth – the notion of how deserving or not you are to receiving something beneficial. It might be a compliment or kind remark in your favour

So, read the full card and then ask your child these questions. Do remember to allow them sufficient time and space to think:

- *Who do you know that is not very healthy?*

- *Who do you know that is healthier than you are?*

- *How healthy would you say you are?*

- *How much do you deserve that health?*

Depending on how positive or negative the answers are, consider asking these supplementary questions:

- *What stops you from deserving the best possible health?*

- *What stops you from deserving more?*

SELF-WORTH
[DESERVING]

11

Do I love and value myself?

I can feel good about myself, and do well in the eyes of others, but I may hide the fact that I am not deserving of success, love and good health, and that this life is all there is.

Self-worth is more resilient than self-esteem, and it may rise and fall over time, depending on how we perceive the world.

When we feel worthy, we tend to make productive choices. When we feel undeserving, we tend to make destructive or limiting choices.

Productive choices bring on helpful, supportive people and experiences, and vice-versa.

When very young, I liked to hear people say they loved me, and mean it. We can raise our self-worth by doing things that serve others, by being kind, helpful and responsible.

Our self-worth goes up when we take ourselves lightly, regard setbacks as lessons, know we are doing the best we can, and maybe realise that this journey has a purpose.

We may also apologise, and ask forgiveness, if only in our mind's eye.

SELF–IMAGE

Your child needs and values constructive feedback – we all do. Feedback affects everything we've talked about including our self–image.

This is perhaps best defined as the way we see ourselves – what picture comes to mind, how we speak to ourselves and even what sense is invoked when we turn the attention on ourselves.

We will all have particular images for how we cook, play football, drive, dress, etc. There are an infinite number of self–images for whatever topics are suggested. This is true even if we hadn't thought about it until now!

Read Card 12 to yourself.

Could you ask your child to read it too?

SELF-IMAGE

How do I see myself?

To see ourselves how others see us...

Our self-image is more than our outward appearance. If we care little about it, we may go through life upsetting others, or neglecting our own well-being. If we care too much, we may become vain and arrogant, or succumb to eating fads to become obese, or painfully thin.

Our self-image is what we see, or think we see when we look in the mirror, it is our self-talk, and how we feel about ourselves.

A healthy and accurate self-image is formed when we use criticism as useful feedback, and reject someone else's attempts to belittle us.

Our self-image stays healthy when we remain open and ask for feedback, especially from those we trust. It stays healthy when we say good things to ourselves, and remain true to ourselves, despite the best intentions of others.

When we see ourselves as [well-intentioned] others do, and combine it with a supportive inner dialogue [self-talk], and look after our bodies, through diet, exercise and rest, our self-esteem and in time, self-worth rise even more.

We might develop this notion of self–image with our child by asking some of the following questions:

When you think of yourself as a:

Footballer, Actor, Painter, Singer, Dancer…

…what sort of picture do you have in your head?

If it's positive you can help them appreciate just how much control they have about how they see and experience themselves. You might find this interesting to try on yourself first!

What happens if you make that picture…

Bigger

Brighter

Nearer to you?

Introduce a piece of inspiring MUSIC!

If it's a negative picture ask:

What happens if you make that picture…

Smaller

Duller

Further away?

Introduce a piece of boring music or no music or sound at all!

What additional questions might you ask?

SELF–BELIEF

Read Card 13.

Our view of ourselves coupled with our own opinion about how deserving we are has a direct bearing on our capacity to succeed.

If my child feels he is a good footballer, likely to score the winning goal – what might his beliefs be? We can only speculate, as it's important to ask, however they might include:

- *I am a winner*

- *I can do it*

- *I know I'm good*

If, on the other hand, our child believes they are never going to be good at art or maths, what beliefs might exist then:

- *I am rubbish at art*

- *I will never be good at this*

- *I hate school*

- *I hate the teacher*

Far fetched? Again, only by asking will we find out some of the beliefs.

Even then it might be difficult to establish what thoughts are there. Observe closely. How does your child hold herself when you discuss this subject? Is she slouched, upright, engaged, disinterested – all these clues will add to the feedback you are receiving.

Try giving a compliment. Does your child reject the remark, pass it off as unworthy? Or do they respond positively, almost preening themselves.

Statements of belief are known as affirmations – things we believe to be true. Unfortunately, research shows that up to 80% of inner dialogue (self–talk), is negative for the average person. Thus it's crucial to start work early on positive affirmations. Try for yourself repeating perhaps a dozen times to start with, some of the following:

- I am a good Dad (Parent/Step–Parent/Grandparent – substitute as applicable below)

- I am a good Mum

- I am great Dad

- I am a great Mum

Notice how different you feel having done this. Now catch your child with a negative belief and convert it into a positive one by asking:

Is there something you believe about yourself that you're not happy with?

e.g. *I am a rubbish footballer … becomes I am a fantastic footballer!*

Keep repeating it – out loud. Look in the mirror and shout it!! Write it down on a post–it note or card, and pin it somewhere where it can be seen and repeated daily. It's thought to take between 21–30 days to change/build a belief. So if practised, within just one month, the change in belief will be noticeable.

This can be done with maths, appearance, art, whatever.

The benefits to self–image, self–belief, and therefore performance are likely to be massive.

Remember to have fun with this particular activity!

SELF–BELIEF
[CAPACITY]

13

How far can I go?

What I believe about myself can propel me to the stars. If I believe I am worthy and competent, and the face I present to the world is my true face, then all that stops me is my imagination.

Beliefs are formed in relation to what I *value*.
If I value honesty, I will believe I am honest.

Most of us have an imaginary ceiling on what we can achieve. Try some of these for size:

- I am capable
- I am worthy
- I am lovable
- I deserve all that life can offer
- I am attractive
- I can do it!

When we can say these aloud, with conviction, and without embarrassment, we are moving rapidly towards our potential.

We can realise that beliefs are the best guess we have about how things are at the moment. We can change ones that don't serve us.

We can forgive our parents and realise they were doing the best they could at the time.

SELF–RESPECT

Have there ever been times when you felt you let yourself down? That perhaps you didn't give it your best shot? Respect is fundamental to all relationships and particularly a coaching relationship.

Read Card 14.

There are many documented cases of highly successful sports teams where members have not liked each other, yet few where there has been a lack of respect for each other's skills. This is so true for the coaching relationship. Respect grows with awareness and coaching is all about raising awareness and encouraging individuals to responsibility. A child or parent who withholds or avoids making connections either through choice or lack of skill in this area is also diminishing respect.

So how can we, as parents, assist in the building of self–respect? The key is to act authentically with your child. This means inspiring through powerful, positive messages. Acting consistently with your own values and being honest.

This will help your child to feel good and eventually your child will start to respect you for this consistency. Now for some parents this will be a more difficult journey than for others. You may fail often. Ask yourself often – "Am I being consistent." Parents who have more than one child will realise the power of this question.

Be strengthened too by knowing that most of us are not born with great parenting skills. They are learnt. So if prior to now you've been inconsistent, here is a useful affirmation.

That's how I used to be ... but not any more!

Self–respect is learnt by witnessing others that you can fully respect too. Once your child knows what that is like, they can start working on it

SELF–RESPECT
[ME & YOU]

14

In respecting myself, I may respect you...

We usually notice when someone has lost their self–respect when they care little for their appearance. Lack of self–respect is about low motivation, low energy and low aspirations, of being easily bored, or not bothered.

Lack of self–respect is a dangerous state to be in, for it leaves us open to exploitation and manipulation.

If we care little for this 'self' we will not stand up for 'ourselves', not bother to maintain it, and even start thinking it may be disposable...

When we respect ourselves, we are proud of who we are, proud of how we present ourselves to the world, and regard this 'self' to be something worth bothering with and investing time and effort in.

We re–gain self–respect when we act in accordance with our highest values or ideals, when we let go of guilt and shame, and when we realise this life, this body, this 'self' is sacred, unique and all we have.

We respect others in the same way we respect ourselves...

REALISING POTENTIAL [1]

Read Card 15.

Consider letting your child read it too.

Ask them:

- *Do you recognise any of the people on this card?*

- *What do you think about the comments made about them?*

- *How might that affect how you think about yourself?*

REALISING POTENTIAL [1]

Aim at the stars and land on the moon...

We are born with immense [unlimited] potential. What limits it?

Beethoven's teacher...
...called him hopeless as a composer.
Walt Disney...
...was fired by an editor for his lack of ideas.
Teachers of Thomas Edison [invented the light bulb]...
...said he was too stupid to learn.
Albert Einstein...
...spoke only after he was four and read after he was seven.
F.W. Woolworth's employers...
...said he hadn't enough sense to wait on customers.
Henry Ford...
...failed and went broke five times before he finally succeeded.
Winston Churchill...
...was poor at English, and bottom of the class.
70 years later he won the Noble prize for literature.

The *potential* we are born with stays with us. We realise it by
listening to our hearts, by believing in ourselves, by helping
others do the same, and by setting outstanding role models for
others, by loving ourselves, and using all our energies to
follow our passion, our destiny.

Realise your potential before it's too late...

REALISING POTENTIAL [2]

Read Card 16.

Ask yourself the questions on the card. This needs to be done in strict sequence.

Write down the answers – be honest with yourself. Remember what we said earlier about respect!

Run this through to the last two powerful coaching questions.

Keep your experience and learning from this card as resources to guide how you help your child realise their own potential.

"...20 years from now, you will be more disappointed by the things you didn't do, than the ones that you did."
Mark Twain

- What are you disappointed about <u>now</u>?
- What talents do you have that you are not using?
- Do you harbour a secret desire to do something, yet just aren't getting around to it?
- How much longer will you deny your potential?
- Who could help you get there?

In your mind's eye imagine yourself as a parent in 20 years time. Can you see what you have achieved? Do you hear others telling you how well you've done? Does this include what a great parent you've been? Are you feeling good about yourself?

So now is a good time to get the answers to these final questions:

1) "How much do you want it?"
2) "What will you give up to get it?"

Exercise Four

Self–Confidence

If you are fortunate enough to have all the confidence you need in every situation, congratulations – it's also unlikely you've learnt anything new. If that's not you, did you note something of worth?

1. _____

_____

2. _____

_____

3. _____

_____

4. _____

_____

Self–Coaching

How will this knowledge affect you?

1. _____

_____

2. _____

_____

3. _____

_____

4. _____

_____

CHAPTER SEVEN

Learning

What is it that makes the human brain so powerful? Certainly it is not the raw processing power of a single neuron within the brain – it takes about one–thousandth of a second for a cell to return to a normal state after firing. While this seems quite a short time it is ridiculously slow compared to even a modest personal computer whose silicon chip can perform operations in the incredibly short time of one–hundred–millionth of a second.

The secret seems to lie in the very *number* of neurons – many tens of billions. If these neurons can be made to work efficiently and simultaneously on a given task then it is clear that the effective power of the brain is very much larger than current computers.

In order for neurons to cooperate in performing some function, they must be able to talk to each other and it's believed that this is enabled through neural pathways. We still have only the crudest understanding of why these neural pathways are connected up the way they are but it is surely the very detailed way in which these connections are made that is at the heart of the power of the brain as a thinking machine.

It has been estimated we only use between 3 and 5% of our brain's capacity, some optimists suggest 10%. In recent years, researchers have found the heart (and other organs) has neurotransmitters, that it has intelligence, and it also sends signals to the brain, rather than merely receiving them.

When a body of knowledge called accelerated leaning, based on brain research is integrated with other cutting edge findings, you have tools at your disposal that will transform the speed and quality of learning and retention.

Where do we begin? With ourselves of course. Simply by making simple mental adjustments, the kind we have been doing unconsciously for years…

Leonardo da Vinci has been consistently voted one of the greatest human beings who ever lived. His range of skills and talent, inventions 500 years before their time, his mental *and* physical prowess, his timeless works, Mona Lisa. He has been studied/copied by a 20th century writer, and one author[9] found that Leonardo used all his senses to learn.

So, if we can discover the secrets of a 15th century genius by copying his likely thoughts and behaviour, just think how powerful our learning can become if we use this approach in everyday life.

Another way of improving learning is to examine different levels of influence. That is, place, time, what we do, what we believe, and our higher levels of motivation all affect our learning. After we have made the best use of all our senses, knowing how we habitually use that information, we can make even better use of it.

The brain organises information though connections, like a web, map or tree. When we make notes like this, we learn and recall quicker. Think about it: which is easier to remember, a picture or pages and pages of text? Want to improve your memory? How are you feeling now? Have you ever used music to help, linking pictures and sounds to the information? Adjust your internal images, sounds and feelings.

---

[9] Michael Gelb [*How to Think like Leonardo da Vinci, pub. Thorsons 1998*]

LEARNING HOW WE LEARN

Whether or not your child can spell well the *way* he knows how to spell can help him learn everything else more powerfully too. If he can't spell too well yet then you'll learn how to improve things on Card 24 in a few pages time.

By learning *how* we learn, we learn *how* to learn how to learn...

Your child does all this without knowing. By allowing him to recognise what is going on, he can not only improve his leaning, but also enjoy life more.

When your child is in the moment, engrossed, ask:

Who are you now? Chances are they will reply, 'me', or with their name or nickname. That's because they are themselves, fully and completely. If you get a negative response e.g. "stupid", "useless" or "bored", you might ask the question again, emphasising the word who. If you still get negative answers, take a trip into self–confidence country.

Card 17 describes three positions:

1. First [when we are ourselves]

2. Second [when someone else]

3. Third [observing ourselves]

The key is to allow your child to recognise the difference, and then ask them to practice each, and then give you feedback. When in dialogue, and your child 'doesn't get it', put yourself in their shoes.

- *What is it like to imagine you are someone else?*

- *What is it like to imagine you are watching yourself?*

Our lives are best lived from the first position.

PERCEPTUAL POSITIONS 17

How can we learn from ourselves?

Do you know what it's like to be another person? Have you ever stood back and imagined you were looking at yourself? We all have.

So, when faced with a tricky task, or learning something 'difficult', put yourself in the shoes of someone you know could do it easily. Become that person; adopt their mode of thinking, reasoning, and making sense of it all.

Ever been in a sticky situation, or again struggling with learning? Just for a moment, take your attention out of your body, and watch yourself. This point may be up, across, or even down from where your 'normal' attention goes.

Finally, when you need your focus and attention in the moment, here and now, be aware of your body, be 100% yourself, notice with your eyes, ears and feelings, what goes on.

Practise these techniques consciously [you have been doing them for years]. Live your life out being here now; observe yourself when you are giving yourself a hard time; and stand in another person's shoes when you need to see things from their point of view.

MAKING SENSE

As Card 18 says, discovering how we use our own senses and becoming an all round learner is a principle and the practice of genius.

Sometimes, we use different senses to remember and to experience. To discover your child's preferences ask:

- *Think about what you are doing now. What is easiest to recall? A picture, sounds, or how you feel?*

This should give you their preference – choose a few examples to be more certain.

- *When you take your mind back a couple of months/years or longer, which comes up first? A picture, sounds, or how you felt?*

This should give you the senses they prefer to use to recall. Whatever comes up, encourage them to use their other senses too:

- *How might you recall pictures/sounds/feelings more?*

Notice by reading Card 18 that our language gives clues to our preferences. Encourage your child to develop their other senses by inviting them with visual (bright, vivid, look etc.), auditory –(tune, hear, listen etc.) and feeling (grip, do, feel etc.) words.

YOUR SENSES
[SEE, HEAR, FEEL, SMELL, TASTE]

18

When learning, what do you pay most attention to?
What you see, hear, feel, smell or taste?

Which sense (or combination of senses) is your
favourite for understanding the world?

It might vary depending on what you are doing, but you will have
a preference. And it may be different from the first sense
you use to remember things.

Do you switch off when asked to watch things? Tune out when
listening to people? Find it difficult to know how you feel?

Learning is best done with as many senses as possible.
The less you use other senses, the more you
restrict your learning capacity.

Ever noticed how you relate best to those who learn like you,
and may not know why you don't like some people,
even though you have no good reason?

I see what you are saying; I'm listening to your point of view.

Discover your own preferences, and then work
out ways to become an all round learner.

This is a principle of genius.

MODELLING

Card 19 points out that we learned to walk, move and talk by copying those who brought us up. This is sometimes called modelling.

It might be no exaggeration to say all learning is modelling. So, help your child model people and actions that are beneficial.

- *I've noticed you X [an obvious behaviour] like me/your mother/father/sister/brother/hero. How did you learn to do that?*

- *When learning by copying others, what senses do you use?*

If they have a weakness or dislike of an important subject, find attractive role models to help them learn.

- *Who is good at this? What do you think you could learn from them?*

- *How can I set a better example for you?*

MODELLING
[BE YOUR ROLE MODEL]

19

Learn only what you want to become...

Remember learning to walk and talk? Before mastering walking, were you ever tempted to give up after falling down too often?

Heard stories about kids who've been raised by wolves and apes? Guess what? They walk and talk like wolves and apes.

Has anyone said you are just like your father or mother? Is it said about your children?

Who are your role models – past and present? What made you who you are today? What makes your children who they are, and who they will be?

We model naturally, instinctively. We copy how others move, talk, hold themselves, learn, breathe, dress, succeed, fail, swear, sing, pray. We model all the time, mostly unaware of what we are taking on board.

So, make a conscious effort to model the best things about the best people you know, and a make the greatest effort in setting an example for your children.

They will always do what you do; they will do what you say when it matches what you do.

LEVELS OF INFLUENCE

Card 20 is awash with powerful coaching questions. Each level of influence has its own question and each is important.

Catch your child doings things right. When they are excelling at learning, discover how time and place influence them:

- *When and where are you at your best?*

When carrying out a task well:

- *What are you paying attention to now?*

When being very skilful:

- *How do you do this?*

Follow up with easier questions about specific tasks.

The "Why" question can often be a double–edged sword. For more in–depth information refer to Chapter Nine – Questioning and Listening. Used as described, "Why" can help you discover your child's beliefs and values.

Again when engrossed:

- *Why do you enjoy this?*

We met the question about identity earlier:

- *Who are you now?*

The implied "Why else" question can also elicit the beginnings of their actual chosen path in life:

- *If you could choose any career, which one would you choose?*

- *If you could do anything in life, whether or not you got paid, what would you do?*

The highest level of motivation often comes when we are doing something for a loved or admired one. Have you ever thought **What** or **Who** are you connected to? Your partner, parents, children, siblings? Maybe friends, community, nature, the human race, church, faith or religion? This level of influence should be used wisely.

- *Who or what might you be doing that for?*

Combining the levels, in a sequence is a highly motivational tool.

LEVELS OF INFLUENCE

20

What or who are you connected to? Your partner, parents, children, siblings? Friends, community, nature, the human race, church, faith or religion?

Why else are you pursuing your passion?

Who are you when you are your best? Have you ever said: *'I'm not myself today'*?

Why do you want your children to be the best they can be?

How do you do certain things extremely well?

What do you do to impress or influence others?

When and where are you at your best?

Are your children in the wrong place and/or time? Does what they are doing need changing? Are they learning how to do the right things?

Do they have supporting beliefs? Are they allowed to be themselves? Why else should they do what you believe is in their best interests? Do they believe in something bigger than themselves?

Just suppose they and you combined the right time and place, with the right behaviour and skills, backed up by conviction, in tune with who you are, and what you are or want to become...

HABITUAL PATTERNS

Card 21 allows you to find out your child's habitual thinking and operating patterns. These patterns are fairly fixed, so help him/her use them to their advantage.

The first seven of the ten questions relates to a range between the two opposites given.

The first question helps find out if your child likes fine detail or the big picture. Enjoying fine detail is necessary in maths and science subjects and for jobs like watchmakers and accountants. People who like the big picture tend to enjoy and excel at art, literature, architecture and dealing with people.

- *When you read these cards, do you prefer the detail, or the big picture?*

Some children like to be given a checklist or a set procedure. Others like to do their own thing based on loose guidelines:

- *When asked to do something do you prefer set procedures, or options?*

We are either motivated *towards* a behaviour (such as winning) or *away* from something (such as not losing). In simple terms, carrot and stick.

- *Which attracts you more – winning or not losing?*

Depending on your child's age, their preference for working on their own on a task or project, or with others, is very valuable for information on their career preferences. It may also highlight coaching needs, as most jobs involve people!

- *When working do you prefer, the task, or people?*

The next one is critical if you find resistance to your praise or feedback:

- *Do you have to have other people tell you that you are doing a good job, or do you just know?*

Those of us who know, don't like being told! And those of us who need to be told can become too dependent on the opinion of others...

The direction of your child's attention may be on themselves or others. If it's the latter, they will pick up non–verbal signals very quickly. So, remember your body language!

- *Is your attention mostly on you, or on others?*

As we've already discovered your child will have specific sensory preferences when learning. And chances are, that for your child to be convinced of something, these preferences are likely to remain:

- *To be convinced of something is it best if they see, hear, touch, read about or do it? And then how often – instantly, over time, after a few more examples, or are they never convinced?*

Many children like variety. We live in a world of sound bites, and rapid change. However as those with several children know – not all kids are the same!

- *How often do you like things to change? Rarely, most of the time, occasionally, or never?*

Ideally, your child responds to stress through choice:

- *When you are stressed, do you get emotional, remain calm and thoughtful, or can you choose either?*

Once you have enabled them to discover their preferences, assist in matching their learning and functioning to them.

WHAT DO YOU DO AFTER USING YOUR SENSES?

21

How do you interpret the world?

When you read these cards, do you prefer
the detail, or the big picture?

Do you prefer set procedures, or options?

Which attracts you more – winning or not losing?

When working do you prefer, the task, or people?

Do you have to have other people tell you that you
are doing a good job, or do you already know?

Is your attention mostly on you, or mostly on others?

To be convinced of something, is it best if you see, hear, touch,
read about or do it? And then how often? Instantly, over time,
after a few more examples, or are you never convinced?

How often do you like things to change? Rarely, most of the time,
occasionally, or never?

When you are stressed, do you get emotional, remain calm and
thoughtful, or can you choose either?

As you have your ways of thinking and
operating, so do your children.

MAKING CONNECTIONS

Making notes of what your children do using Mind Maps – Card 22 – can present a challenge at first. Mind maps were developed in the late 1960s by Tony Buzan[10] as a way of helping students make notes that used only key words and images. They are much quicker to make, and because of their visual quality much easier to remember and review. The non–linear nature of mind maps makes it easy to link and cross–reference different elements of the map. There are many excellent books on the subject, and many schools now teach this technique.

- *What subjects/ topics/ things are better understood using Mind Maps?*

- *How can you realise even more the value of Mind Maps?*

---

[10] To discover more visit the Tony Buzan website – http://www.mind–map.com

MAKING CONNECTIONS

22

Ever thought of making notes like this?

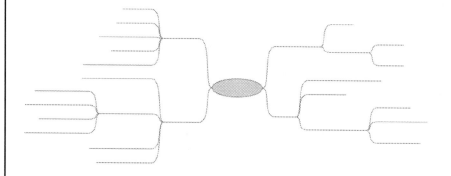

Mind-maps 'model' our brains. Our brains think in pictures, and make connections between what we see, hear and experience. Learning to use mind maps will transform your learning of information, ideas and concepts.

Persist with this new way of recording information, as it may take a little time to re-adjust.

REMEMBER MORE

Card 23 lists a series of techniques that will improve recall. Questions that accelerate their learning include:

- *When learning, how might you attach an emotion to important information?*

- *Allow yourself to relax, letting your mind help you remember…*

- *What kind of music might help you learn better?*

Want to remember musical scales? Music students know, "every good boy deserves favour" is a mnemonic phrase (EGBDF) to remember the treble clef.

Numbers? 1 – Candle, 2 – Swan and so on.

When being introduced to someone for the first time, repeat their name out loud, so that you hear it. Now imagine their name written on their forehead so that you see it. If you can without drawing attention to yourself, write their name in air with your finger or hand, so that you 'feel' it.

- *When you think of X, what do they look like, sound like, feel like?*

- *Make X's face bigger and more colourful. Move it around. Attach your favourite music to this image…*

REMEMBER MORE [1]

How can I improve my memory?

How much of what you want to remember
has an emotional charge attached to it?

When your memory stalls, what state are you in?
Tense, anxious, relaxed, or confident?

Remembering information, or facts and theories depends
on how effectively you absorb it, how well you order it,
and then how well you recall it.

Learn to speed read – improve your absorption.
Play Mozart or Baroque music as you learn.

Organise what you're learning by using Mind Maps
[see Making Connections – Card 22].

Associate words with a story and numbers by
associating them with pictures to improve recall.

Recall faces in at least three senses. Where in your
mind's eye do you store things you remember easily?

Experiment with the size, colour, and location of
your internal images. Add your favourite music.

Make what you want to recall big, colourful and bright.
Want to forget? Make them small, dull and distant.

SPELLING STRATEGY

How do you and your child know how to spell?

As for the previous card, Card 24 contains techniques. After teaching these techniques, check out the recall by asking:

- *What words, which you previously weren't sure of, can you now spell?*

- *When you move your eyes up/left/right/down, what comes to mind?*

See the card for:

- *How can you make success at exam or tests more real?*

REMEMBER MORE [2]

How do you know how to spell?

Good spellers see the word in their mind's eye.
A good feeling confirms it is spelled correctly.

If your spelling is [in your opinion] poor, then
you may be 'sounding the words out.'

Improve your spelling by reading a correct version, look at it, and
then move your eyes up the left [if this doesn't work try up to the
right]. Feel good because you know it is right.

When wanting to spell it, recall the image. Try the word in
different colours. You will be able to spell any word using this.

To recall words or music, look across to your left
[some may prefer right]. Recall feelings by looking
down to your right [or left].

Recall pictures or diagrams by looking up.

For exams or tests, visualise the test centre. Notice what you will
be doing. Think of skills you use to pass the test. Believe you
deserve to pass. You are the person who passes the test.
The test is one of your life goals.

Associate passing the test to the people,
or things you hold most dear...

IN CLOSING...

Whilst we learn though modelling, learning is also 'state dependent.' That is, when we are relaxed, alert, focused, optimally stressed and free from negative effects of food or drink, we excel.

One last point, sometimes the left side of our brains [which are overused when we learn facts, information and make 'normal' notes] don't connect as well as they should with the right side of our brains, which engage when we draw, create, paint etc.

- *How can you learn without effort?*

- *What can you do to use everyday occurrences to help you learn more?*

- *How can you link movement with learning?*

Education kinesiologists[11] have created a whole range of movements that quickly integrate left and right brains. Jack Stewart has also written *Moving For A Change* (also with Bookshaker.com) which will be available in 2006. It contains 36 ways you can use movement from stillness to riding a bike to change your life.

---

[11] Kinesiologists study the factors that influence human movement and look for ways to improve the efficiency and performance of the human body at work, in sport and in daily life.

Exercise Five

Learning

Are you still learning or are you beginning to suffer from a 'hardening of the attitudes'? If you have gained something from this topic write in here exactly what it is.

1. _____

_____

2. _____

_____

3. _____

_____

4. _____

_____

Self–Coaching

What will you do differently as a result of this knowledge?

1. _____

_____

2. _____

_____

3. _____

_____

4. _____

_____

CHAPTER EIGHT

Coaching

Coaching is a relatively new profession. One way to understand coaching is to think of it in terms of outcomes. In other words, start with the end in mind. If we know what we intend to accomplish, we can correct ourselves as we go along and be able to evaluate our success at the end.

Coaching is quite different from counselling or consulting. It is rarely concerned with the past, spending little time talking about, "what if" and "maybe someday." It is focused on improving performance, and helping others to 'succeed' at something that is important to them, and sometimes to you as a parent too.

Relationships will often improve. A child being coached will usually begin to speak with greater clarity, and act with more confidence and power.

Interestingly, it's possible to even coach your child before it even enters the world! "How on earth can that happen?" you might reasonably ask. There is evidence that raising awareness in the child whilst it is in the mother's womb is both possible and desirable. Studies have compared brain cell growth in children stimulated in the womb with those who were not. Whilst further research continues and there is debate, it seems that brain cells increase in stimulated unborn children. In those having no particular attention during pregnancy, numbers of brain cells reduced in some cases by up to 50%.

How does this relate to coaching? Apply a simple regular coaching exercise once the mother becomes aware of movement within the developing baby. For example the baby may kick or stretch on one side of the mother's stomach. At this point send a clear and simple response to the child, by for example tapping a set number of times on the same area of the stomach. This needs to be a consistent response such as two or three taps, to every one push or stretch from the child. The aim is to create a feedback loop, where the unborn child becomes aware that so many pushes produces a set response. A word of advice though: keep your responses absolutely consistent so that the learning is established. Have fun with this, and do let us know of any particular experiences you may have!

DISCIPLINE

To achieve anything worthwhile discipline is vital. Have you ever started something yet not finished it? Have you ever meant to get started but somehow never did?

What's often missing is simply repeating the actions that need to be in place to allow you to succeed. If we accept this to be true, then it's our responsibility to help our children understand the role of discipline.

Read the whole of Card 25 through.

Consider the last line. Is it a risk you are willing to accept?

Decide now – when the going gets tough…

"I will exercise the necessary amount of discipline, no matter how difficult."

DISCIPLINE

25

Dare to discipline – your child depends on it!

Do you remember as a child how easy it was to outwit some teachers, because sometimes they let you get away with something on one occasion, but not on another?
Did you or others push them to the brink?

As a parent are you sometimes like some of these teachers? Being consistent in what you say and do is what's needed. As is knowing where you stand on a particularly difficult issue. Although it might not always seem so, a child naturally craves standards, discipline and predictability to provide a sense of security.

So what is a parent to do? Discipline your child in the early years, when there is hope. Say "No" when you know it's best for him/her. Don't be open-minded all the time. Use the wisdom you have been gaining over these years to make decisions in their best interests.

If you don't, <u>you</u> [not your child], risks ruining their life.

GOAL SETTING

First read Card 26 right through.

I'm constantly fascinated when I talk with children, that in spite of all the popular talk about goal setting, very few actually know where they want to get to[12]. These same individuals are usually crystal clear on what they don't want.

Yet life is totally consistent – whatever we focus on for long enough will eventually come into our reality. So if we constantly repeat, "I don't want X", the probability is that 'X' will very soon appear! In essence negative talk is actually negative goal setting.

Discuss the Lewis Carroll lesson in this card with your child.

Ask yourself… "Do I really have goals for the things I want to achieve in my life?" If not, why not? What's holding me back? Is the fear of failure perhaps in there?

If you are serious about coaching your child to success, how useful might it be to consider your own position on this?

Now – write down a few challenging things you'd like to achieve in the rest of your life. It can be anything:

- A brand new car
- A dream holiday
- Learning to paint
- Taking up dancing

You set the standard. You must write it down. Great – now you are ready to have a conversation with your child where you fully understand the subject and can walk the talk.

Remember a goal is a dream with an action plan attached to it!

---

[12] "Alice's adventures in wonderland", Lewis Carroll 1865

GOAL SETTING

26

Do I know or like where I'm going?

> *"Would you tell me which way I ought to go from here?" asked Alice.*
>
> *"That depends a good deal on where you want to get," said the Cat.*
>
> *"I really don't care where," replied Alice.*
>
> *"Then it doesn't much matter which way you go," said the Cat.*

Lewis Carroll, Alice's Adventures in Wonderland.

What sort of goals do you have? How will you know when you get there? Will anyone else be involved? What does accomplishing them mean for you?

You see, without considering these points, the likelihood is that you might just as well go with the traffic flow even if that's on the road to nowhere...

PRINCIPLES

How do you stop doing something when you don't know you are doing it?

You probably had to think quite hard about that question. Of course you can't stop doing something you don't know about. The same is true about the reverse – doing something that may never have occurred to you. Getting too difficult?

Read the card now.

Can you now understand how your awareness[13] has just changed as a result of reading that card? Yet, you did not know that it needed to change, did you? This is true of our interactions with others, and therefore with our exchanges with our children.

Your job is to raise your child's awareness of the impact they have through either doing or not doing something. This isn't about pointing something out through saying, "You always do that" or "You never do that." It's a great deal more subtle.

Try this:

- *What effect do you think that has on how well you do?*

- *How often would you say you did that?*

- *Have you ever considered what that might mean to your friend?*

You might just try these questions on yourself.

By raising awareness the next piece of the coaching jigsaw drops into place. It's called responsibility. Once you become aware of something, you at least have the *option* of owning it. It becomes a choice.

---

[13] Adapted from many sources including 'Coaching for Performance' Sir John Whitmore, pub Nicholas Brealey 1996

PRINCIPLES

27

The essence of coaching is about raising awareness and responsibility in the individual. Your intention with your child is for them to become empowered to do what until then, they might have believed impossible.

Help your child understand that they are OK [completely functional] and don't need fixing and that they already have all the resources they need. Your sole (soul) purpose is to help discover the responses that will 'raise their game' to a higher level [enhanced function] and even beyond to excellence.

The breakthrough for your child will occur at the moment they realise that they are empowered to take charge of their own life.

LISTENING

Are you a good listener? How do you know? Do you really concentrate when someone is talking to you? Have you peeked ahead at the contents of this card? What distracted you – it's not easy is it? There are many potential distractions. The one thing you can be certain about is that your child will spot if you are not giving them your wholehearted attention.

So what should we do? Have a full read of the card now.

The keys to good listening are contained in those last emboldened words. Engaging yourself in the conversation will help greatly in your child's recognition of how involved you are. By constantly confirming your own understanding you also will *feel* more involved. At that point your relationship will move to a new and higher level.

LISTENING

28

Did you say something?

Whenever you really listen to your child's comments, your reason for doing so is to understand – to enter as much as possible into their world, to listen with your heart and gut as well as with your ears and brain.

To listen actively means that while you're taking in what's being said, you're not busy evaluating, judging, blaming, interpreting, thinking about how you're going to respond, speculating about where the conversation is likely to lead, letting your mind drift to the next TV programme, or the meal that needs cooking.

Instead, focus entirely on what you're receiving to appreciate where your child is coming from, how s/he feels about what s/he is saying, why s/he feels that way, and what the meaning of their words are to them and their life.

To show you are listening and understanding fully, test constantly:

'As I understand it … Is that right?'
or
'So what you're saying is … Is that what you mean?'

SELF–COACHING

Would you like to coach yourself? The best way to find out is to give it a go! So how does one get started? First decide, what is it you want to work on. The reason for this is simply to get the topic or situation into the open, where it will be easier to clarify. For example: "I want to help Tom to improve his maths homework marks."

Study paragraphs three and four on the card. Paragraph three is about how you might like things to be. Paragraph four is about how things actually are right now.

Now depending on a variety of factors you will find this next part may work better one way than it does another. Sometimes it's easier to explain what it is we don't want, than what it is we'd really like.

None the less, comparing the two parts will produce greater clarity. So in the ideal world I want Tom to find his maths homework easy to do. Yet the reality might be that he hates doing his maths homework and struggles to get started.

Now read the paragraph starting, "Wonder what I could do if I didn't have to answer to anyone?" Remember this is you coaching yourself – you are not coaching your child at this point. Possible answers might be:

- "I could hire a tutor for my child."

- "I could sit down and read the homework with him."

- "I could have a word with his teacher."

The more you practice speculating as to what you might do, the easier it becomes. It's now essential that a timescale is set, otherwise you might never achieve a beneficial change.

This principle of self–coaching is the identical one for coaching your child. The only difference is that your child becomes the first person.

Specifically, "Tom, how might I help you with your maths homework?" Reply, "I would like you to help me understand it better…"

Just take it from there and share ideas, options, and possibilities. Be gentle with yourself, let your child lead and don't expect to be perfect at the beginning. Practice is what's needed.

SELF-COACHING

29

How do I get started?

With this situation? Perhaps it would help if I were to question myself? After all, I'm pretty good at asking others the hard questions!

Well, "What exactly do I want to work on?" – so now it's got a name.

In my ideal world "What do I want to be, do or have?" Now I have an idea of what it might be like in the future. In fact, this tells me "How I will recognise success – can I measure it?"

Hmmm – "What is happening now that tells me, that bright new future isn't yet here!" May as well hear the truth...and there's no point lying to myself is there?

"Wonder, what I could do about things if I didn't have to answer to anyone." After all I'm the only one listening...actually I'm sure I can think of plenty of ideas.

I feel I am getting somewhere – but by when? "Yes, exactly when do I want to have sorted this...?" If that's the case "What's the first step I will take?"

Now I'm on the path...

Exercise Six

Coaching

There are numerous styles of coaching, all having their own merits. Expert or novice, what have you found in this Chapter that you can apply?

1. _____

_____

2. _____

_____

3. _____

_____

4. _____

_____

Self–Coaching

What will you do differently as a result of this knowledge?

1. _____

_____

2. _____

_____

3. _____

_____

4. _____

_____

CHAPTER NINE

Optimising Stress

We all know that too little stress is as harmful as too much, and that one person's trauma is another's irritation. So, in life it is a question of *optimising* stress, rather than removing it.

Another issue is how we use our energies and what we apply effort to.

Most of us are conditioned to accept that to achieve anything, we must work 18 hours a day, seven days a week, and in so doing, stretch and strain every muscle. Hard work of course never hurt anybody, but blind application of effort without rest and recovery is useless, and even dangerous.

As we get older, our attention, which as children is mostly on what we are doing, i.e. in the moment, gets more and more focused on the past or the future. Being in the moment liberates us from fear, and is the place from which success springs.

What we eat and drink is another matter of increasing importance. We hear of conflicting opinions about most things, but there are certain truths about 'food and mood.'

We all have a basic daily regime of getting up, washing, eating, drinking and relieving ourselves. Without this discipline, life would be impossible. So, how about extending this discipline to quieten the mind, copy the habits of successful people, find a domestic refuge, a private mental oasis in our busy lives?

How many times do we curse ourselves, and say things to our kids we regret afterwards? Well, if you knew what harmful words did to people, you might start using praise and love a little more often.

Perhaps this chapter can be summed up by spending more time listening to your heart, and less time in your head. Again children do this naturally, it is up to us to help them return to their own inner wisdom.

RELAXING

Being a child, your son or daughter probably has masses of energy. You will most likely 'relax' differently. It is very hard to expect your child to learn relaxation, unless you do.

Clearly there is nothing wrong with conventional ways of relaxing. However, excepting perhaps the bath, most of them do not truly allow you to relax.

Does your child see you as relaxed or tense?

- *How do I come across? As someone who is relaxed, and takes things in their stride, or tense, angry, or stressed?*

- *What do you notice about me that makes you say that?*

If the guidelines on the card prove a challenge, why not join a local yoga class, invest in some tapes, and learn how to meditate?

Watch your child for a few days and noticing how she relaxes. Then ask:

- *What do you do so that you wake up refreshed?*

- *How important is it for you to slow down a little during the day?*

Isn't it wonderful that your child can show you a few things?

RELAXING

30

When do you truly relax?

Is relaxing watching the TV, drinking a glass of wine, reading a book, or easing yourself into a hot bath? Try this. First put aside some time when you will be undisturbed.

Sit, or lie down, flat on your back, with warm clothes if the room is cool. Breathe deeply, letting the air you breathe in inflate your chest, and deflate breathing out. Imagine every in breath is pure, soothing clean air; every out breath releases toxins, or tension. Begin with your feet, and continue up the whole body. Tense your feet, then release. Tense your legs, then release, etc. Go mentally to your favourite place of relaxation. Dwell there for a while.

If tense, ask yourself silently: 'Will the part of me that helps me relax, please communicate with me now?' Notice your feelings.

In your actual place of relaxation, play soothing music. Burn candles/incense sticks safely.

Pills don't make you fit, and it takes time. True relaxation is as necessary as effort, for without it, burn out or serious illness beckons.

Practice relaxation, watch your output increase, your health improve, and your life blossom.

How has your child relaxed today?

BEING PRESENT... NOW

Card 31 is about returning to the moment, and quietening the mind. In your child's case, it is about helping them stay in the moment, and developing positive self–talk, and letting go of any self–doubt.

Find out how your child stays in the moment. Discover what they say to themselves when they do well, and then not so well.

Firstly catch them engrossed in an activity they love:

- *What are you noticing/ hearing/ feeling/ thinking when you are doing that?*

And then:

- *When you have done something you feel proud of, what do you say to yourself?*

- *What other situations might you do better in as you remind yourself of the good times?*

Take the answers, reflect on them, and ask:

- *How can we help each other stay in the now?*

BEING IN THE NOW

31

In the past regretting; in the future, anxious...?

As we age, the time consciously spent in the moment decreases.
As young children, our attention is on what we are doing now.
We want them to think about the future, they want
to think about the now.

We fill our heads with problems; hear all about gloomy
or wonderful futures. If our now is difficult, thoughts
return to better days.

Self-talk takes us from the now. In the now we
heal/excel/relax/create. We find our true selves.
We are human beings, not human doings.

It is important to plan, to work towards goals. The past still has
many lessons for us. Focusing on important targets moves us
forward. Find a sense of proportion. If we spend 90%+ of our
time in the past or future, we may wake up one day and wonder
where our lives have gone. Ever seen an epitaph that reads
'Wanted to spend more time at work'?

Like relaxation, all this requires practice. Watch your offspring
lose themselves in the now. Ask how they do it,
encourage and model them.

How much have you been in the now today?

FOOD & MOOD

Unless your child has been taught nutrition, and even then, we know much of it is conflicting, it is sufficient to get them to realise that what they put into their bodies affects them. The greatest service you can do here is to help them educate themselves to recognise stress signals from the body. Then you can both ignore much of what passes for 'advice.'

Check out each of the points you regard as relevant:

- *How do you feel <u>just after</u> you have just drunk/eaten product X, Y, Z?*

- *How do you feel about <u>fifteen minutes</u> after you have just drunk/eaten product X, Y, Z?*

- *What food is most helpful for you before or when learning?*

And, if you know one of your child's role models eats well:

- *What kind of things does your [sporting/acting/singing] hero eat?*

Allowing your child to discover that their outer (self–created) world reflects their inner world will go a long way to their acquiring empowering habits for life. It might just get that room tidied up too!

FOOD & MOOD

32

Does what you eat add to your well-being?

We live in a world full of contradictory information. One person's health scare is another's lifesaver. Yet certain things are fact.

- Food alters our mood.
- We lose weight by eating less.
- Exercise is good for you.
- Sugar can give you an energy 'spike' [boost] followed by a lowering of energy levels.
- Smoking kills you, and prematurely ages skin.
- Sugar is in most prepared food.
- Artificial sweeteners aren't proven to be safe.
- Diets don't work.
- Leonardo da Vinci [probably the greatest genius who ever lived] was a vegetarian.
- Food advertising promotes unhealthy diets.
- We need 6-8 glasses of water per day.

At school [and often at work], vending machines sell food that is full of sugar and/or fat. Learning performance is often impaired by simply what we eat.

Aggression, being passive, high, low or 'normal' can be 100% through what we eat.

A school virtually had no discipline problems with water coolers available in all classrooms.

Make the right food choices for your family.

DAILY DISCIPLINE

Check out Card 33. It's probably fair to say that just about anyone who is successful has exercised self discipline.

Before addressing this subject, do some homework. Find out whom your child admires, and then bring the matter up in conversation. If their role model is completely ill–disciplined, try another approach (see below).

- *How much might you benefit from being more like [their hero]?*

Of course, 'more like' in this context is discipline:

- *Were you aware they spent 1 hour a day meditating, praying or visualising – or whatever you select to serve as a good habit?*

Alternatively, you could invite them to spend their daily routine with you:

- *What might we do together every day that would help us both?*

Then collaborate!

DAILY DISCIPLINE

33

Is chaos outside reflected in chaos inside?

Untidy rooms, houses, cars, appearance, are visible reminders of an undisciplined/chaotic inner world. Daily routines promote inner discipline, inner order.

Our minds wander off in a stream of random thoughts when we lose concentration. Daily routines of exercise, relaxation, even prayer or meditation, promote inner calm and inner harmony.

Successful people have discipline.

In a world of constant change, discipline is our rock, our friend, and our one certainty.

Typical, real life examples:

- Standing or sitting meditation
- Yoga, Tai Chi, Chanting, Singing
- Running, walking, bike riding
- Exercise machines
- Sitting and relaxing
- Practicing any sport or hobby

Free up 5–15 minutes every day? [0·3–1% of your time]

Set an example for your children by setting an example for yourself.

MESSAGES FROM WATER

You might also use Card 34 to help your child drink more water...

The learning is for you to stop using hurtful words to them, and vice-versa, and for them to stop doing it to others.

The book[14] is a good bet or ask them to explore what it feels like when they hear certain words:

- *If anyone calls you something negative, what does it feel like?*

- *Where in the body do you feel it?*

- *You might remember being called this before. Your mind remembers, is it possible the body might store it too?*

Use the messages here to help them expand their responses to insults and conflict. Help them develop more choices.

- *What else might you do rather than call them a worse name back?*

---

[14] Messages from Water, by Masuru Emoto, pub. HADO Kyoikusha Co. Ltd

MESSAGES FROM WATER

34

What vibes do you give out?

Our bodies are 75% water [brains over 80%]. The moon and planets influence the tides. Self–evidently, that which influences water, influences us. Music and sound can seriously change our moods. This much we know.

Research proves music can help plants die, grow quickly or slowly, or thrive.

Experiments conducted in Japan have led to amazing discoveries. Photographs were taken of frozen water just before it melts. Remember the beautiful shape of ice crystals in winter? The Japanese studies show water, in its crystalline form being subjected to different kinds of music, and different kinds of words. When water is subjected to hateful words, it becomes distorted and ugly. The opposite happens with kind and loving words.

'Sticks and stones may break my bones, but words will never hurt me.'

Our very being distorts with unkind, hateful words.

What kind words have you said today?

HEAD & HEART

Read Card 35.

Some people believe that allowing the heart to rule the head is giving in to temptation and a recipe for self–indulgence.

If your child discovers their talent for listening to their heart, you will worry less about them trusting the 'wrong' people, following the 'wrong' direction in life, and doing the 'wrong' things.

- Ideally, your child will be good at head activities – thinking, planning, logic, analysing and heart – creating, dreaming, dancing, expressing.

- *When faced with two choices, what helps you make the right choice for you?*

- *How do you know you have made the right choice?*

And when they tell you, say to them:

- It is important to think things through, and it is just as important to do things we feel are right. In what ways will 'listening to your heart' enable you to make even better choices now?

If our destiny is to become the person we dream about, encourage them to dream whilst injecting some realism, including boundaries too:

- How can you listen to your heart, and your head?

HEAD & HEART

35

Which serves you best, your head or your heart?

The hardest journey? From our heads to hearts.

Research has proven the heart [and other organs] have neurotransmitters, i.e. they send messages, as well as receiving them. When your heart [your inner knowing, not the desire to do something reckless] says one thing, your head the other, what do you do?

Our heads decide, and our hearts choose.

Our education system, is about left–brain, head thinking. 'Dyslexic' children, gifted in art, music & dance, happy in the now, lose out. TV quizzes, testing knowledge and recall, abound.

It is not a question of head or heart, but the integration of both. 'Success' is more than test and exam performance. So pay attention to head and heart.

Decisions bind us, choices can liberate. Help children to decide and to choose. Choosing is the consequence of living in the moment, and listening to our hearts.

Help your children set boundaries, and let them help you go beyond yours.

IN CLOSING

Stress is a question of perspective, or for the auditory learners the right note, and for kinaesthetics perhaps a vibe.

- In what other ways might you now use stress to your advantage?

- How can you stay 'cool', or whatever the 'in word' is, and optimise your stress levels?

- How can you help your friends to become less stressed?

Adopt a lifestyle that optimises your stress levels. Would you like your child to model tension?

Exercise Seven

Optimising Stress

Stress is a modern day term. What does it mean to you and specifically what have you taken out of this topic?

1. _____

_____

2. _____

_____

3. _____

_____

4. _____

_____

Self–Coaching

How do you think you and others will benefit from this knowledge?

1. _____

_____

2. _____

_____

3. _____

_____

4. _____

_____

CHAPTER TEN

Jokers

Read the story of Chris – Card 36.

Did it in any way resonate with you? How much do you think your children love themselves? What would they say if you asked them?

There is a school of thought that says we can never express an emotion to someone else more than we do for ourselves.

For example... Have you ever known someone who didn't really feel confident, and that person was always dragging others down, to their level?

CHRIS

36

Chris, a retired midwife, bore scars of ignoring her own needs.
She came for help. Ashen-faced, moving awkwardly,
with no zest for life.

I was directive [avoiding a slap!]. "If I asked you
if you loved yourself, what would you tell me?"

"Love myself? My job was to love my mothers and
their babies. Love myself? It's ridiculous."

Weeks later, finding out she had Parkinson's Disease
[like boxer Muhammad Ali], Chris finally realised she couldn't
help anyone until she devoted all her energies to herself.

After months of medical and therapeutic help, Chris
has learned healing, started going to the gym again,
and had an insatiable thirst for learning.

Very occasionally she returns for therapy. Seeing her recently,
I couldn't believe the changes. Positively glowing, no longer
the shell of a person who had struggled into my office
a couple of years ago.

Despite having advanced Parkinson's Disease, Chris says: 'There
are good days and not-so-good days - but then doesn't
everyone get the same?' And: 'I have been given my life back.'

Learning to love yourself is the greatest love of all...

Perhaps for a significant example, think of Mother Theresa. She knew the love of God was so total, that she was able to pass that on to everyone she met. No one ever doubted her sincerity.

So this comes back to all those early ideas of self–esteem and self–image. Try this thinking on for yourself. Maybe just for today, decide you will be very confident. Notice how that thinking then affects others around you, in a positive way.

Caution yourself that if you wake up in a bad mood, about the effect that will have on others around you.

Ask your child:

- "Do you love yourself?"

If they say no, ask two questions:

- What would it be like if you did love yourself?
- What would be different?

You will note a positive reaction. Now suggest:

- How about just for today and for a bit of fun, you act as if you really love yourself?

When that day is over, suggest they try again the next day, and so on.

THE JOY OF ILLNESS

Read Card 37.

How are you today? Great thank you? Not too bad? Not so good? Whichever it is, we all love some form of acknowledgment don't we?

Would you be surprised to learn that the greatest act of growing into a mature human being is to relinquish completely the need for the good approval of others? Interested? Try it just for a day; go through a whole day doing good things without needing the attention of others. It's the most empowering experience you could ever have.

How does this relate to children? It's about acknowledging them. Loving them, yet letting them know that they're not to make a career out of being ill. They're to aim to be the best they can be – regardless.

Who is the real you? Have you ever found yourself acting in a particular way or saying certain things, just to impress others? If you have, you're like most of us. However the greatest learning is the point at which one learns to accept oneself – warts and all.

THE JOY OF ILLNESS

37

'Kneelock' makes a career out of being ill. In common with another local luminary who uses a psychiatrist to re-confirm his unwell status, both have no incentive to become well.

Kneelock's personal illness 'kit' is jars of tablets, a neck brace, walking stick, and a motorised wheelchair. Dressing glamorously, she cuts a dash with high heels, neck brace and stick when she trips to the pub without her 'chair.'

Illness brings both of them concern, compassion, and attention, even though it is not always favourable.

To become well would be their undoing. Both work [in varying roles] by the way, in case you might be thinking they are lazy.

Unwell children learn that mum or dad brings treats. We love Lucozade, a warm bed, and even being in a different 'state' for a short while. Most of us associate illness with being pampered and freedom from adult pressures.

Despite the charms of being fussed over, and being the centre of attention, most people prefer wellness.

For those who prefer a career in illness, do you wonder how they ever managed to make the 'wrong' choice in the first place?

YOUR TRUE SELF

Read Card 38.

Now ask your child:

- *Do you ever say things to try and impress your friends?*

- *Have you ever?*

If they can't or don't admit to this behaviour, volunteer something about yourself – about an occasion when you may have done that.

This is a great exercise in learning to find and accept your true self.

JOEY

38

At the end of a programme for 14-year-old lads in the Midlands, I heard something that changed my life. The programme was an attempt to change the behaviour, and offer some future, to young men two inner-city schools found almost uncontrollable.

Unlike the boys' hard-pressed teachers, a colleague and I had the luxury of decent surroundings, comfortable chairs, hot drinks on tap, and interesting exercises. The 'naughty boys' were still very *challenging.*

One of the quieter lads, Joey, had an uncle who hated him, and kept saying he was useless. No one at home stuck up for him. Joey himself, like his mates, wore clothes way past their best. He also had a real quick wit and dry humour. With considerable intelligence neither measured nor valued by the system, Joey intrigued me.

We handed out a questionnaire, asking what the lads wanted out of life. We got the usual mix, *'footballer,' 'successful', 'own business', 'married with my own kids', 'working with computers'.* Heart-warming stuff.

I asked Joey if he would show me his paper, as he had written something different on his. He read out, with no hint of embarrassment:

'I want to find my true self.'

ROLE MODEL

Read Card 39.

What do you understand by the term role model?

When you were growing up did you ever have anybody in your life that you regarded as a role model? Perhaps with the wisdom of hindsight you now realise that somebody was in fact a role model for you.

If this is true then what effect do you have on your children? How do they relate to you? How might your behaviour, attitudes and beliefs, be affecting their impressions of the world? Of adulthood? Has the reverse ever been true? Do you modify your behaviour based on how your children behave?

Powerful stuff isn't it?

SAMMY

39

Sammy, an adorable black–and–white cat, was blessed with special gifts. After his unexpected and distressing death, it was apparent what his presence brought to our house.

What price a creature who loved you unconditionally, and would always greet you with a purr and friendly rub against your legs as you came though the door? Like most animals, if all was not well, he would soon sense it, and pay you even more attention.

What qualities do we value most in our friends, children, partners and friends?

Honesty, loyalty, kindness, sensitivity, reliability, compassion, playfulness, the joy of life?

The Cat Shelter staff confirmed Sammy had been ill treated by his previous owners. When he first came to us, he took an instant dislike to one of our other cats. Had we got it wrong?

Before long, Sammy's true character emerged. He had all the qualities above and more. Sammy would befriend anyone who came to our house – yes, even if *we* didn't like him.

My wife and I like to think Sammy modelled his behaviour on us. But, to this day, we can never be sure whether we modelled our behaviour on him...

NOT BAD?

Read Card 40.

Remember the *Why Else?* question from Card 20?

Do you believe there is a purpose to your life or do you just stumble on day after day?

What do you think your children believe?

How do you know?

Have you ever asked them? Why not?

Have another read of the card.

Now consider, if you have an idea what your life's purpose is, how many things have you done today that contribute towards you achieving that purpose?

How much time and energy have you wasted on things that have absolutely nothing to do with achieving that purpose?

What would it be like if you had known at the earliest moment exactly what your purpose was?

What would you have done differently?

What would you keep doing?

How might you share this conversation with your children?

If this strikes any chords with you then surely your responsibility as a parent is to share it as quickly as possible with your child?

Help them to know that what they think, say and do counts – everything.

YOUR LIFE PURPOSE

What is your life purpose?

Is it what you make it, or does some unseen force, or being, decide it for you? Did your own child come complete with instructions, like a packet of seeds, as to what they will become?

A friend, Jeff, and I had two very similar experiences – in supermarkets of all places.

We swapped our brains for the trolley, and were slowly, aimlessly wandering around the aisles, silently cursing others for doing the same.

My wife spotted an old friend. She had not seen her for over 20 years. Brightly, she asked: 'How are you?' The reply came wearily, slowly and depressingly back: 'Well, I'm *still here*.'

Jeff spotted two people asking of each other's health. He overheard one say: 'Well, I'm still *above ground*.'

So, when asked how you are, and you reply: *Not bad*, or *could be better*, think for a moment about this life of purpose – your life. If your child adopts a resigned outlook, rather than one of joy, what message are you sending out?

Whether it's down to you, or an unseen force, aren't you capable of something more than *'not bad?'*

THE SAME STREET

Read Card 41[15].

What do you think this story is about?

How does it relate to how you've lived *your* life?

What might you do differently now you know this story?

How will you explain the principle to your child?

How about asking your child to explain the principle back to you?

What might be good about that?

---

[15] With acknowledgements to Portia Nelson – ''Autobiography in Five Short Chapters''

MY AUTOBIOGRAPHY IN FIVE SHORT CHAPTERS

Chapter I: I walk down the street. There is a deep hole in the pavement. I fall in. I am lost... I am helpless. It isn't my fault. It takes forever to find a way out.

Chapter II: I walk down the same street. There is a deep hole in the pavement. I pretend I don't see it. I fall in again. I can't believe I am in this same place. But it isn't my fault. It still takes a long time to get out.

Chapter III: I walk down the same street. There is a deep hole in the pavement. I see it is there. I still fall in... it's a habit... but, my eyes are open. I know where I am. It is my fault. I get out immediately.

Chapter IV: I walk down the same street. There is a deep hole in the pavement. I walk around it.

Chapter V:

I walk down another street.[1]

WHAT YOU HAVE WITHIN...

Read Card 42.

This is a profound story, but what's the message?

What part does greed play in the story? How relevant is it that the stone is precious? What valuable thing have you ever given away? What value does the wise woman place on the stone? Is envy a feature of the story? If it is, what exactly is being envied?

Have you ever wanted something that wasn't yours in your life? How might it have helped you not to have done so?

What will you now say to your child about your learning from this card?

THE WISE WOMAN'S STONE

42

An old, wise woman who was travelling in the mountains found a precious stone in a stream. The next day she met another traveller who was tired and hungry, and the wise woman opened her bag to share her food. The hungry traveller saw the precious stone. In a flash, he asked the woman to give it to him.

She did so without hesitation. The traveller left, rejoicing in his good fortune. He knew the stone was worth enough to give him security for a lifetime.

However, a few days later he came back to return the stone to the wise woman.

"I've been thinking," he said, "I know how valuable the stone is, but I give it back in the hope that you can give me something even more precious..."

"Give me what you have within you that enabled you to give me the stone."

YOU CANNOT FAIL

Success, is a great word isn't it? It's interesting too. If I said to you, "what has been your biggest success?" You would probably think of something, given a little time. Try asking your child that question – after you've read the card – resist any temptation you may have to influence them.

The concept of success is wrapped up in many different things.

Maybe try asking your child some additional questions:

- *Who do you regard as successful?*

- *What makes them successful?*

- *What do you think they have done that has allowed them to be successful, or enabled them to be successful?*

This is a great opportunity to involve other ideas from other cards.

Having goals, recognising the role of failure, knowing where you are today and where you want to be in the future.

Perhaps greatest of all, really understanding the meaning of the statement, "There is no failure, only feedback."

- *What would you do if you knew you couldn't fail?*

Ask your child that question. Be prepared for some fascinating answers.

SUCCESS

43

It was the first day of our 'Modelling Genius' course for boosting self-confidence of inner city kids. Twenty-two young people, anxious but excited, they felt special to be chosen from hundreds of others.

An average school career lasts for around 1,000 days. These kids were getting four days on something that could turn their lives around.

The first question we asked was: "Tell us something you feel proud of – success – something you have achieved."

After a long silence, thinking they didn't want to appear smarter than their friends, we asked them to write down what they couldn't say. Half an hour of cajoling and persuading later, a handful of them got the idea. It wasn't shyness; they had no idea of what success and pride meant. We were shocked. This was challenging! So we decided to keep giving frequent opportunities to succeed.

By the last day of the course they realised success was to draw wonderful pictures, to play an instrument, nurse family members, win competitions outside school, rear animals, stop smoking, get on with previously hated teachers, and to learn new skills and knowledge.

What has your child succeeded at today?

TOMORROW

Pause for a moment, and on this occasion, *read all of the text below* before reading the card on the next page!

Have you ever known exactly the right things to do and exactly the right things to say but when you did them they didn't work? It's a bit like having a recipe, doing everything right and the cake flops.

One of the great things with coaching is to create an atmosphere of future expectation. It's done with the simple statement:

- *"What are you most looking forward to about tomorrow?"*

It pre–supposes a number of things:

- *That you are looking forward to something.*

- *That you are looking forward to more than one thing.*

- *That the future will indeed be positive.*

And even though you may not have thought of something, the statement forces you to comment on the fact that there will be something you can look forward to. So – a very powerful statement. Enjoy the card.

CHARLOTTE

A client decided to follow up on some coaching ideas to help prepare his daughter to positively anticipate the next day. In his words...

Day 1

Me: "What did you most enjoy about today?"

Charlotte: *"Not sure–can I tell you what I least enjoyed?"*

Me: "OK."

Charlotte: *"The dodgem car crashing into us and making me bang my head and also the fireworks were too loud."*

Me: "What are you most looking forward to tomorrow?"

This gets a big smile and lists the next day's schedule – the morning at tennis classes, lunch at TGI Friday's, picking up friend Georgina and going to Top Golf. She settles down to sleep happy and contented with life.

Day 2.

Me: "What did you most enjoy about today?"

Charlotte: *"Why do you always ask me that?"*

Me: "What are you most looking forward tomorrow?"

Charlotte: Growls, *"I'm not looking forward to you asking me these questions!"*

Day 3.

Me: "What did you most enjoy about today?" earns me a growl.

Me: "What are you most looking forward tomorrow?"

Charlotte: "Hitting you if you ask me this again!"

Day 4.

I should have seen this coming. "What did you most enjoy about today?" earns me the customary growl and...

a not particularly gentle thump!

Have a read of Card 45. What did you learn?

Dyslexia (pronounced: dis–lek–see–uh) is a learning problem some youngsters have with reading and writing. It can make words look jumbled. This makes it difficult for a child to read and remember what was read.

It's not to do with intelligence either. In fact, some very smart people have had dyslexia. Albert Einstein was dyslexic.

The problem does occur in the brain, though. Sometimes the messages the brain is sending get jumbled up or confused. A child who has dyslexia might get frustrated and find it hard to do schoolwork. The good news is that dyslexia doesn't need to keep a child down.

Referring back to the card – which came first? The bullying or the dyslexia?

- *How might one reinforce the other?*

- *What happened after Sam started to regain or perhaps gain self–esteem?*

- *What might this tell you about the importance of that subject?*

- *What questions might you ask your child as a result of your learning here?*

- *What might you ask them about their impressions about other children? Especially those who appear less able than they are?*

SAM

Amongst my first clients were two lads who were being bullied at school. Bullied because they were 'dyslexic', and therefore different.

Both parents were dyslexic. Their father had been badly injured at work, and was recovering. The legal minefield of compensation for his accident would daunt anyone – for them it proved too much. The family missed out on £1000's.

The lads were wonderful young men, one a talented musician, the other a skilled artist.

Ten–year–old Sam, was unsure about his future. His ambition? A world tour in his dad's old motor home.

I got his confidence, then we worked through spelling strategy. [See Remembering More (2) – Card 24]

When he came he could spell virtually nothing. Two sessions later he could spell any word in the dictionary. He was ecstatic. His confidence grew visibly. More self–esteem work followed. He wanted to *learn* again.

Asked about his career choice after the last session, he said: "Marine biologist."

I saw him a few years later, when he was fourteen. He was taller than me [6' 3"], and solid. I suspect the bullies had faded away...

<u>Exercise Eight</u>

Jokers

Stories tell us a lot about others and especially ourselves. What have these 'Jokers' reminded you about yourself?

1. _____

_____

2. _____

_____

3. _____

_____

4. _____

_____

Self–Coaching

What will you do differently as a result of this knowledge?

1. _____

_____

2. _____

_____

3. _____

_____

4. _____

_____

CHAPTER ELEVEN

Case Studies

LEARNING

This case study concerns two examples of how coaching can pay off. Both concern learning and self–confidence. We all know from our own school days, how an inability to learn seriously affects our confidence, and of course vice–versa.

Nuala, a bright, engaging, energetic nine year old, is the daughter of a friend. Her parents are very keen for her to do well at school, and her father was once one of my students; he knows much of the material in *The Coaching Parent.*

She goes to a good school, in so far as the head teacher and his staff are dedicated and able. There seems to be little tension amongst the pupils, and there is an active Parent Teacher Association.

Yet, despite her proven intelligence, she was struggling with English and later maths. Her mother told me about her poor marks in English, and how she was in danger of being classified as a slow learner. Her reports bore this out, which meant that:

1) The teacher and the school had yet to find out her learning preferences – which suggested the subject was being taught in one way only, and those who learned this way would be the best students.

2) Nuala had not yet found out she could adapt her learning to suit the way the subject was taught.

A few years ago, Jack was invited to speak at a large conference for early years teachers and assistants. The town that hosted it had a deserved national reputation for innovation and achievement in the field. His topic was learning preferences. After talking about the three primary senses (see, hear, feel) and getting the 200+ people on board, he decided to ask them all which sense they preferred to learn with. About 100 hands went up for visual (see). He usually next asks about auditory (hear), but his instincts told him not to. How many kinaesthetic (feel) learners? Another 100 hands. He was shocked, and a buzz went around the room. So, what did that leave us with? Two auditory learners! Allowing for any shortcomings in his presentation, it was still dramatic proof that teachers, even in progressive LEAs, have much to do to teach the way kids learn...

So, on this occasion, I thought the best approach was to ask Jane, Nuala's mother, some questions! It soon became apparent that Nuala made pictures in her head (a visual learner) and had not found ways to connect what the teacher said.

The teacher's internal world was auditory and as you might imagine, we teach how we learn. I suggested Jane try asking Nuala to experiment with what came to mind when she spoke to her. Did the sounds in Jane's head match the pictures in Nuala's? If not, what could Nuala do about it? A separate approach to the teacher concerned had revealed what I suspected – she could only teach the subject one way – great if you learned like her?

So she practised, with Jane's help, how to connect sounds and pictures. For example, the teacher said 'lawnmower', assuming everyone knew what one *sounded* like. What did it *look* like? The other boost came from rejecting the slow learner label. Aren't even the most able amongst us slow at some subjects and fast at others? Nuala's confidence grew. A few weeks later she was one of the top pupils in the subject.

The same applied with maths where there was a mis–match between the teaching and learning. I discovered the way I learned to multiply was not the way Nuala did. Her way was quicker, the school's methods were better! I found she was learning faster than I could understand.

Again, a combination of trial and error, supportive questioning, and a desire to find out how she actually learned all paid off. No more problems in maths.

I was left with further proof that much of the problems with teaching kids *anything*, is that they learn faster than we do. Approach them thinking, "They already know *how* to do this, it's just that they might not know *what* it is." This is much better than, "How can I transfer what's in my head to theirs?"

How can your child help you become a better learner and teacher?

RAPPORT

This case study describes one of my first brushes with coaching. When, in my therapist mode, a mother brought her 10 year old son, Paul, to me as she was concerned about her relationship with him.

It was obvious straight away that the lad and his mother adored each other. I was puzzled as to what the problem might be, if indeed there was one.

If coaching is about enhancing performance, as opposed to digging out problems and solving them, I learned it that day.

Paul was understandably wary of yet another authority figure. I assumed, possibly wrongly, that the school featured in this somewhere. He showed me a letter he had written to his mother.

My personal priority was to build trust (see Card 1) and rapport (see Chapter 5) as quickly as I could. The mother didn't seem awash with money, and why should she pay for any useless attempts at getting the lad on my side?

How do you do this? I felt a deep compassion for the lad, a burning desire to be of help, one that respected (See Card 2), empowered him, and confirmed to him his own self–worth. I also paid great attention to his body language or physiology (see Card 3)

Is it that simple?

A wonderful model, which I was introduced to in therapy, captures this perfectly. Working one–to–one with anyone, we have two indispensable resources – the <u>*heart and the sword*</u>*. This book, the questions and the tools in here and elsewhere, are the sword. The heart is our compassion, or love for the person. One of the technically best and most intelligent people I have ever met – a world leader in his field – suggests we go for the heart every time.*

Paul showed me his letter, which had the potential to move me to tears, but I don't think he would have appreciated me crying, and pointed out a few spelling mistakes. To me, they were unimportant, to him however, *as he had mentioned them*; it's obvious they were. So I asked him what the longest word in the English language was. He didn't know, but the question had hooked him – the unspoken message was wouldn't it be great if you could spell that. I was busy 'pacing and leading' (see Card 8) throughout.

Whether 'antidisestablishmentarianism' still is the longest word in the English language I don't know.

I had guessed correctly, he wanted to be able to spell better. I had no idea about other aspects of his relationship with his mother.

So, all my previous therapeutic stuff went by the wayside. We spent 15 minutes with the 'spelling strategy' (see Card 24). The rest of the time was spent convincing him it was no fluke. It wasn't. He knew it wasn't.

In coaching him to spell the above 28–letter word, his self–esteem shot through the roof.

Paul and I shook hands. His mother asked me what had happened, and I asked him how he now felt about spelling. His mother was amazed…

What might you do to improve rapport with your child? Maybe raise your own self–esteem and learning while you are at it?

SELF–CONFIDENCE

This case study shows how trainers and teachers can adopt a coaching style with students/pupils, and the rewards that follow.

Colleagues and I were presenting a programme at a West Midlands school, and we were all impressed by the commitment of one of the young Asian students (Malik) to use the learning to improve his life chances.

He made great progress throughout the five days, yet something appeared to be pre–occupying him. My wife, Anne took the trouble to ask him if he wanted to talk about anything.

After some reluctance Malik opened up. His family were to go to France later that year, and would be visiting some of the war graves. He was dreading it – the thought that he wouldn't be able to cope with the emotions it would stir up in his family and himself.

"So you want to go to France, and are looking forward to it, yet the visit to the graves concerns you, is that about it?", asked Anne.

She knew from the odd comment he had made over the last few days that he was worried about getting upset. To ask outright might have embarrassed him, so she said: "If you could change anything about the visit, what would it be?"

"Well," said Malik, "I'd rather not go to the graves, but I know how much it means to my dad, so I guess if I could stay calm and confident during that visit, I'd be raring to go."

"Like the time you did that exercise last week?", said Anne, knowing he had shone at one particular task.

"You bet," he said.

So, she had discovered the obvious, a time in his life he had been exactly in the frame of mind/state to cope with adversity. Indeed, when he had pleasantly surprised himself.

"What do you remember about feeling confident?"

"How good it felt."

"Where in your body are you feeling it most now?"

"It's like a warm glow in my chest."

"And if you let it get warmer, stronger, spreading through your whole body, how would that feel, now?"

"Great!"

"And if you were to think about the French trip, what had you been worried about?"

"I was bothered about visiting the graves, but now it's no big deal, in fact I'm looking forward to it, 'cos I know my dad has wanted to go for years. I can't wait."

The principle involved here is that a strong positive feeling or state always pushes out a weaker negative one, especially when the person really wants it. Malik wanted to go to France for many reasons himself, and yet wanted to do it for his dad which was his greater motivation. Tapping into a previous memory of confidence and adding his strong motivation gave the anxiety about the visit no chance at all.

How might you raise your child's self–belief by helping them overcome a problem?

OPTIMISING STRESS

An associate, Jeff Moran, runs programmes in schools, helping teenagers with their learning and self–confidence. When he gets the chance, Jeff goes into overdrive about stress. In fact he covers much of the material presented on Cards 30–35.

Jeff's passion is sound. He recently told me about the effect of different music on mice – although we do not condone experiments that cause animals suffering.

Mice were given a task under 'normal' laboratory conditions, then the same task, with different kinds of music played to them. The time to complete the task was massively reduced when baroque/classical music was used (see Card 34). And when 'rock' music was played? The mice started to kill each other!

Working in schools brings me in contact with some remarkable kids. In fact, a goal I only recently revealed to my sponsors when working with a group of 14 year olds was to get them to be silent for 1 minute. A few years ago, I found this an almost impossible task, despite my world class, cutting edge rapport skills!

It may be obvious, that all these case studies are difficult to separate out into distinct categories. If you hate the teacher and lack rapport then learning is a problem; if you hate yourself and lack self–confidence then antisocial behaviour can become the norm; if you are pre–occupied emotionally or physically stressed then, by definition, your attention is on what occupies you! Whether our kids have been labelled (ADHD etc.) or stigmatised, or are 'normal', matters little. Unless stress levels are enabling rather than disabling, kids like Ken (the hero of this case study) have few options open to them.

Ken is dyslexic, or does he just learn differently? His mother noticed a big difference with him after he began to take relaxation seriously.

Ken was finding it hard to concentrate on any of his school work, and his mother thought there would be no end to her going in to see his teacher about his progress. Homework was always a struggle for him too.

Whilst I wondered about his diet (see Card 32) I've realised that there are many ways to getting kids off junk food and addictive sugar spikes from sweets and fizzy drinks, but I didn't think Ken would welcome this direction. A similar argument applies to personal discipline (see Card 33). Ken had great difficulty in relaxing. After a few minutes of our talking I found out he liked listening to music.

His mother told me that if he calmed down then the whole house would benefit. So, he actually wanted to relax, was de–motivated and stressed at present, and had several options open to him.

Relaxation can be described, but it is best experienced. So, I asked Ken to try out a particular relaxation CD. He agreed to do so before he came back. This is what his mother had to say:

"Over the last few weeks his whole attitude has changed, he does his homework, he is taking more pride in himself and his appearance, he is more motivated and more importantly he is happier. He will not go to bed without the CD. The CD has also had a calming effect on the rest of the house, the kids go to bed no bother, and just nod off to sleep."

I wasn't bothered whether Ken had decided to meditate, have relaxing baths, or buy a decent CD. I'm glad he didn't choose to drink wine, or worse, as he was only 12!

This was another case of establishing trust and respect, then pacing and leading to build rapport, listening and finally helping with generating of options. These are all at the core of coaching.

All just to get him to relax!

What do all world class people do when they are not performing? Have sessions of world class relaxation!

How might you provide your child with a model of relaxation?

CHAPTER TWELVE

Worked examples

In Chapter 2 we introduced the four conversations between parent and child, which highlighted certain areas. As you now know only *you* can decide whether to help your child in the moment, or if you need to set aside a time specifically for something which demands more serious attention.

It is self–evident to us that many, if not all, of you will have had similar conversations, without labelling them in any way. Indeed, you may have read them and said, "That's just common sense."

Even though it may be, could you do this for everything your child brings to you? Could you have similar conversations consistently? Does what works for one of your children, work for others? Do you know what enables you to be a good coach?

By adding the last column 'What the parent thinks' to the dialogues, we are offering you the opportunity to step into the coaching mind–set for different situations, to do it consistently, and eventually to 'coach' without being aware of it for everything your child will bring to you.

You may also begin to notice how the GROW model informs each conversation.

#1 – RAPPORT

Crucial in communication, children instinctively notice its presence or absence. The GROW model elements are highlighted in **BOLD**.

Parent says...	Child says...	Parent thinks...
	Mum, why is it sometimes easier to get on with Dad than at other times?	
What do you mean Josh?		Check Josh's **R**eality
	Well there was a problem yesterday, didn't he tell you?	
No – go on ...	*Dad told me off for dropping my dinner off the tray.*	
So you lost rapport?	*Rap what? What's that?*	
Sorry, yes it is a strange word isn't it? Well – let me put it another way – how do you know when you are getting on with someone?	*Don't know – it just sort of clicks I guess.*	

So when Dad told, you off what was it like?	*Awful. He shouted, which I didn't like. Then he swore, which made it even worse as he never swears. Not only that, but the carpet was a horrible spaghetti Bolognese colour!*	
...then what happened?	*I said sorry – it was an accident. He wasn't happy though and made me clean it all up. He was grumpy for ages.*	
	Later on I asked if he wanted a cup of tea and he was a lot nicer – like normal really.	
How could you tell?	*He smiled and he said "come here" and gave me a cuddle. He was okay after that.*	
So you were back in rapport?	*If that's what that word means, yes I guess so. It seemed more comfortable, almost as though it had never happened. Is that what rapport is then?*	

That's exactly what rapport is like.		
If something like this ever happened again, and I hope it doesn't, what might you do differently?		Help generate **O**ptions and **W**hat will you do
	I'd apologise straight away – then say don't be cross with me for ages, as I feel uncomfortable when you do that.	
How would dad take that do you think?	*Don't know – he might be alright, he might not.*	
What could you do to find out?	*I could ask him before it happens, so that he knows I don't like it!!*	**W**hat will you do
Interesting idea, when would you do that?	*Tonight – but before tea!*	
How will you know if he's happy with that?	*If he is understanding, then I'll know I've cracked it!*	That's the **G**oal

#2 – SELF–CONFIDENCE

The degree to which we react to events, are committed to a particular decision, or a course of action, is directly affected by our self–confidence. The GROW model is highlighted in **BOLD**.

Parent says...	Child says...	Parent thinks...
	Mum, why am I so clumsy all the time?	Wonder what this is about?
What have you done Jessica...?		
	I've just knocked my homework books on the floor. Yesterday I knocked a cup over!	
Just because you did that doesn't mean you are clumsy does it?	*Well I think it does!*	Check Jessica's **R**eality
Jessica, it is likely if you keep insisting that you are clumsy, that soon you are going to believe it.	*What do you mean?*	Let's intercept this potentially negative pattern...
Well – just for fun, can you imagine what the very opposite of clumsy might be?	*Don't know – how about not clumsy?*	Help generate **O**ptions
Well that's true, actually I'm wondering if there is a positive way of saying that? At the moment you are saying **you're not** something. How about **I am** something...	*Don't know what the opposite is – how about graceful? No that's not me either!*	It's important to generate a positive state of mind

Okay let's try going with that just as an experiment. How would you feel if you were graceful?	*Confident I guess.*	
And if you were confident, how would that be?	*Good!*	
Does a confident person ever knock her books or drinks over?	*I wouldn't think so, and even if they did they probably wouldn't worry about it.*	Check Jessica's **R**eality again – no–one is perfect!
Well why don't you try that? In your minds eye imagine you are that confident person – how is that?	*…Its cool. I'm aware of everything around me. Yet, it's all under control.*	
How good is that?	*Its great – I'm really confident.*	
Great stuff – just remember this moment, as you go on from here – whatever happens you are that confident person!	*Thanks Mum – you're a star!*	That's the **G**oal and **W**hat will you do – combined

#3 – LEARNING

Lessons and homework – the topic of learning is common for many families at tea time. The GROW model is highlighted in **BOLD**.

Parent says...	Child says...	Parent thinks...
How's it going Josh?	*Terrible, I'm just rubbish at maths.*	Yikes – I was rubbish at maths too!
		Big subject – best narrow it down!
Surely you can't be rubbish at all of maths, is there anything in particular that's difficult?	*Well I guess its algebra mostly. We've been doing it for weeks now and I just can't get the hang of it.*	Yikes – I was rubbish at algebra too!
		I must avoid passing my concerns on – I won't call it a problem.
What's happening with algebra then?	*It just doesn't make sense at all*	Okay – let's get some structure into the way I help Josh...
Is there any of it that does make sense?	*I think I know how simple equations work*	Check Josh's **R**eality
Anything else?	*No that's about it, I can't do quadratics though*	Hmmm – yes I remember the name and it still means nothing to me either.

		Let's start building the future.
How do you want to be at algebra?	*I need to understand quadratics.*	
And if you did, what would be happening?	*I'd be getting good marks.*	Right – let's establish exactly how Josh is doing.
What are your marks like now?	*I get about 40% right.*	
Well you must be doing something right then!	*I suppose so.*	Raise awareness of current success.
What sort of marks would you be happy with?	*I'd like to get at least 70% right.*	Now we have a **G**oal
I wonder what you might do to improve – have you any ideas?	*Not really.*	Josh has lost confidence and probably interest – let's get some **O**ptions going
Well to be honest maths wasn't a strong point for me either. However I do know something about working these sort of things out.		Keep rapport

If you were being really creative, like you are with English, what sort of ideas would you come up with?	*Hmmm...* *Well I could ask to sit with David, he seems to understand this stuff. I could ask Sir if he would give me a hand, I don't like asking in front of the others though. And I could ask for some old maths papers to practice with.*	Remind Josh of where else he has succeeded – it's only algebra where there is currently a challenge to overcome.
Great stuff – which of those do you prefer?	*I think sitting with David, he is really good, but I don't think he'll mind helping me a little bit.*	Any ideas must be fully owned by Josh
Okay – when will you sort that out?	*Tomorrow I'm going to ask Chloe – she's his sister – to have a word with him because she knows him really well and she likes me!*	I must resist stating "ask him"... however it's key to have total clarity about **W**hat <u>Josh</u> will do now. It's about ownership.
		Point proven – he knows the best way!

#4 – OPTIMISING STRESS

With children, and teenagers in particular, the simplest things can often lead to stress that might be out of proportion to reality. The GROW model is highlighted in **BOLD**.

Parent says...	Child says...	Parent thinks...
Hi Emily, how are you?	*Don't ask!*	Yikes! Best tread carefully...!
		Wonder what it is – boyfriend trouble I bet!
Give me an idea, I might be able to help.	*Doubt it...*	This is going to be hard going...
		I must avoid passing my concerns on – I <u>won't</u> call it a problem.
Shall I start guessing or will you give me an idea?	*Knowing you if I don't give you an idea, you are just going to nag me to death!*	That's right!
Don't be silly – go on, I'm listening...		Check Emily's **R**eality
	It's Becky.	
What about her?	*She is such a pain, I'm sick of her, she drives me mad!*	

How does she do that?	*Whatever I say she says, whatever I wear she wears, wherever I go she goes – I want to strangle her!*	Must stay out of the content, – avoid judging.
Is there a reason she does this?	*No she is just stupid and it stresses me out!*	
I'm wondering if there might be a reason and it's just that we don't know it yet.	*I don't care and what's it got to do with you anyway?*	I've said 'we' to avoid saying 'you' – Emily doesn't miss a trick. I'll still ignore that remark!
It seems to me that if you didn't care, you wouldn't be getting so stressed out.	*Maybe, maybe not.*	Now we are getting somewhere – she is feigning indifference.
How would you like things to be with Becky?	*I'd like her to go away, so that I don't feel so stressed!*	Now we have a **G**oal – it needs testing though.
Does she know that?	*Not really, I just ignore her.*	
How do you think that makes her feel?	*Probably pretty bad I guess – it's her own fault though.*	Now Emily is putting herself in the other person's shoes – we are getting somewhere.
Do you really want her to go away?	*I do if she keeps being so stupid.*	So now it's conditional?

What do you think she wants?	*I've no idea and I don't really care.*	
How could you find out?	*Oh! I suppose I could ask her.*	What a good idea!
Just supposing that you did, what might be good about that?	*She might tell me why she is being such a pain…*	This might be the **W**hat to do – now wait for the full answer – give her time to work this through.
…Anything else?	*I would probably feel a little better just knowing why she is driving me so crazy!*	She now knows the benefits of these **O**ptions and has reasons for this revised **G**oal.
We started by wanting to reduce your stress – I get the idea that talking to Becky would be worthwhile, what do you think?	*Oh you drive me mad too – of course it makes sense. Thanks Mum!*	
Will you sort it soon?	*Yes, I'll talk to her – and you – tomorrow. Are you happy now?*	Job done!

Exercise Nine

Worked Examples

Have these examples cleared up the mystery of coaching for you? Make a note of any particular breakthroughs.

1. _____

_____

2. _____

_____

3. _____

_____

4. _____

_____

Self–Coaching

When exactly do you intend to implement these learnings?

1. _____

_____

2. _____

_____

3. _____

_____

4. _____

_____

APPENDIX

FREQUENTLY ASKED QUESTIONS

1. I have the physical cards which pre–date the combined book and CD – do I still need this book?

It all depends... if you are confident in your coaching ability, then probably not. However, if you would like to deepen and expand your coaching performance, it can only help. The CD contains the cards in an animated format and the cards are a physical pack of 45 cards – you may find either or both as a useful alternative.

The cards and/or CD are available via our web sites:

http://www.thedirectorscoach.com   http://www.organisationalhealing.org

2. How can coaching help my child from being bullied?

Depending on when and where the bullying occurs, that's an issue that must always be taken up with the school or the bullying child's parents. A child with low self–esteem will often be bullied and to help deal with this our book has a dedicated topic – Chapter 6 – Self–confidence. Over time this will help your child gain many of the resources needed to deal appropriately with the bullying.

3. My child shows no interest in school or learning of any kind. Any suggestion of 'coaching' is met with a sneer. What can I do?

As you know, this book is about helping you coach effortlessly. Mostly your child won't even know it. However, we are not naive, and it won't be long before your child (or children) notices something is different – they might even find the book, cards or CD! So how about encouraging your child with the idea that all top people have a coach? Whether they are interested in tennis, football, rugby, cricket, singing, music, dance, politics, whatever. Then they should be aware of the benefits this brings in building excellence in performance. And you know, don't you, what their interests are? How might you help them become who they want to be?

4. **My son/daughter seems to resent any attempt on my part to help using coaching. Their view is, "You don't understand what I'm being taught at school, so how can you help me?"**

It's possible to help, as you won't be teaching. As we mention later (question 5), teaching is primarily about imparting knowledge. As the coach we don't especially need detailed knowledge of school subjects. Coaching starts from the position that the person being coached already has the answers, not necessarily of the subject matter itself, but of the wider issues involved. This is because it's their experience you are working with and not your own. Thus it's geared towards helping to elicit ideas and options from the person being coached – not about you being the expert who needs to know everything. It is possible that you can provide the benefit of your knowledge gained over the years. However, this may only be done once you have exhausted all the good ideas your child will reveal during the Options phase of coaching – refer to Chapter Four – GROW Your Kids! Make sure you gain permission from your child first that it's okay to make suggestions during that phase.

5. **All this 'coaching' is a way to compensate for poor teaching. If they had good teachers, doing their job properly, none of this would be needed.**

Teaching is primarily about imparting knowledge. Coaching starts from the position that the person being coached already has the answers, but may not realise, and getting them out may be more difficult. Thus it's geared towards eliciting the answers from the person being coached, not about you being the expert who imparts knowledge. Although please note our answer in question 4 above.

6. I can't spare the time to coach. I work full time and have to do the housework and care for my children when I get home.

You won't need any more time in order to coach. It is about finding opportunities. At any stage you can invest as much or as little time in preparation as you are able. Some people work on a single topic e.g. optimising stress and keep going with that until they are happy. Others pick a card for the day or the week and work solely on that. So you really can go at a pace that fits your lifestyle. There is a strong possibility that as you discover how easy it is to do you will find more time to coach rather than less. That more of your time is being spent coaching rather than less just because it is so rewarding.

7. My son/daughter is more interested in going out than their future. Having a good time is what she wants, not vague promises of a better career.

As coaching can help with goals of any kind, including leisure as well as work, you will be able to help them make more informed decisions in those leisure areas that they are most interested. By taking this approach the child is likely to become more aware of the impact of their inattention to school work through the coaching dialogue.

8. The school tells me my child is a bully/always in trouble/keeps missing lessons. How can coaching help?

As children don't easily see things from another's perspective, they may need help in this area. A good way of keeping kids out of trouble is to get them occupied with other things. It's important to establish a hobby, sport or other interest if at all possible.

Another important aspect is to establish clear moral guidelines from the beginning. Its not always easy for children and time invested in teaching them clarity over right and wrong is never wasted. Imposing stricter discipline is a challenge for many parents, yet it does help the child to have clear boundaries.

We have a complete chapter on rapport which includes coaching on putting yourself in the 'other person's shoes'. Additionally, we include a chapter on making learning more relevant and interesting, which may encourage your child to appreciate learning in more resourceful ways.

9. At what age should I begin coaching my child?

Originally we thought *The Coaching Parent* would start at any time from about 5 years onwards. How mistaken we were! A parent has since told us of the successes gained with their 3 year old as a result of *The Coaching Parent* approach. So now we wonder what use it is to have any lower age limit and there's certainly no upper limit!

10. Are there better times during the day or evening than others to coach?

Whilst there are no absolutes, there are suggestions as to the best moments. If either party is very tired, overly stressed or just not in the mood then this may have a bearing on the outcome. We don't stick slavishly to this point as both of us have many experiences of coaching children in these situations, and by the end of the session the child is in a totally different energised or positive state. Practice will help you realise when the best time presents itself.

11. I will find it difficult to discipline my child if they see me as their coach. Aren't the two roles incompatible?

There is no incompatibility as your intention is to become the best possible parent. This parent has coaching skills amongst many other qualities. You won't be asking your child to perceive you as their coach and therefore the act of discipline remains available to you.

12. I'm not a very confident person. Although I get on very well with my son/daughter, I find it hard to be a decent role model.

No need to worry – ask your child to nominate a role model they aspire to and then refer to the chapter on learning, where there are many cards that will assist you and your child. You might also find the self–confidence chapter of benefit. By coaching well, you will become confident in that aspect of yourself, and it won't be long before you start to realise that as you become more confident, so does your child. Few of us were born with confidence – it is something we learn.

13. My son/daughter doesn't need coaching. In fact, they could coach me.

That's great news as you will both benefit. Coaching is about taking the person from where they are now to a further place of excellence. All that may differ is the perceived starting point for each of you. Remember: top performers in any field have coaches to move them on to another level. Encourage your child with this information.

14. We have four children. How on earth can we find the time to coach them all?

How about coaching the eldest one and encouraging them to coach the next one and so on? That way you become a coaching family!

15. There is no suitable place in our house to do any coaching. We are always likely to be interrupted.

Coaching doesn't always require complete silence or a special place. There may be things that you prefer to have privacy over during conversation. However most sessions can be held in a room or outdoors with other people in or around. I (David) have held coaching sessions where I've gone for a walk with the person I'm coaching. Those of you who enjoy a walk will know the conversational value of these activities with partners, friends, family, children ...

**16. My husband helps coach football with the boys at school –
won't he know this stuff already?**

There is little doubt he will know how to coach sport! One of my
business clients coaches his local team of youngsters. We've discovered
this is entirely compatible and complementary with his background. Our
material covers areas many parents are unlikely to have come across, and
even though in this instance your husband may help the boys with self–
confidence, he might pay less attention to rapport, learning and
optimising stress. The approach is different as sport is a unique context,
and an extremely valuable one. So just imagine how good he, you, and
your children will become when these skills are added to your repertoire!

**17. One of my children is no problem for me, yet with the other
one everything is a challenge. Will the book be able to help me
with these different situations?**

What an opportunity! So, one of your children is clearly coping well with
life, and your other hasn't cracked it yet. The book will help you discover
how your 'successful' child operates, and how to assist your other child
in learning to develop his or her skills and strategies. Let us know how
the 'successful' child does it and we may, with your permission, use them
as a case study…

**18. Our school/church runs parenting classes, so what's different
with this book?**

We start from the premise that you already have all the resources you
need. Parenting classes can be very useful and may provide other wider
learning. In our experience, they often give sound advice about tackling
problems and common issues. *The Coaching Parent* is about helping your
child realise their potential. Go to the parenting classes *and* read the book
– become the best parent you can be.

19. I find relating to my stepson is very difficult – how will your book help me with that?

Jack has two stepdaughters, and three step grandchildren. He loves them all dearly. However, when he first met his step–daughters over 20 years ago, he knows had he been more of a Coaching Parent then, the relationship he now enjoys would have come about much sooner. Rapport is the key to all of it. David as a father of two and grandfather to two has different experiences and also agrees that rapport is the significant factor.

20. Isn't it the case that most people struggle with how best to discipline their children? Wouldn't more emphasis on assertiveness for parents be better?

Assertiveness may be regarded as a win–win relationship, having your needs met, whilst helping your child meet theirs. Like parenting classes, the skills and knowledge can only help. We feel that a parent who can coach, has learned rapport skills, knows how to help build confidence, optimise stress and assist the learning process will function at a much higher level than merely an assertive one.

21. My teenage daughter and I can't have a conversation without arguing. My partner says we're just too alike. If that's the case is your book going to be of any use?

What does 'alike' mean? What a gift. Maybe you both are proud and independent people? If you are alike, then what would happen if one of you became more aware, sensitive and skilled at relationships? Suppose it was you. Your daughter would unconsciously model you, and learn these things herself. How then could two aware, sensitive relationship experts argue? The discussions you will have will be so productive…

ABOUT THE AUTHORS

DAVID MISKIMIN

Executive and Business Coach, Consultant, Trainer, Keynote Presenter, Radio Broadcaster, Author and Writer.

David, founder of **The Directors Coach,** is an Executive and Business Coach with a background of over 15 years senior management experience within ICL, NorTel and Reuters. David works as a coach and mentor with people at all levels and with teams in business. His own understanding as a senior manager enables him to help senior people achieve performance excellence. This includes CEOs, MDs and Lawyers. He has a particular passion in the building of purpose, direction and follow–through with senior teams. His coaching clients include financial services, engineering, software and consultancy companies as well as the public sector.

Coaching Academy trained, David is a Founder Member of (what is now) Coaching and Mentoring International, contributes to their Corporate Coach Training and is dedicated to the development of coaching. They commissioned David to write the communications module of their first Corporate Coaching Programme. EEF (the UK organisation for engineering, manufacturing and technology based businesses), commissioned David to write and deliver to its members a Managing & Motivating programme and modules for the Institute of Leadership & Management Diploma. He is retained for ongoing delivery of these and other programmes.

As an accredited trainer, consultant and coach, he holds LCA, MCLC, British Psychological Society Level A and B, Assoc CIPD qualifications, Myers Briggs and 16PF practitioner and is an internationally accredited NLP Practitioner. Trained by the Dale Carnegie Organisation, David achieved awards for Outstanding Performance and Human Relations. Committed to life–long learning, David is undertaking the Noble Manhattan Coaching post–graduate Corporate Coaching Practitioner Diploma (Masters level).

A popular keynote speaker, he has appeared on BBC Radio Stoke, Merseyside and Manchester for interviews and phone–in coaching, and has a regular newspaper column. He joined forces with Jack Stewart in order to provide younger members of society with a means to realise their talents.

David is married to Laura. They have two daughters, Nicole and Anne–Marie, and two grandsons, Marcus and Aiden. Contact him through email to david@thedirectorscoach.com.

JACK STEWART

Psychotherapist, Author, Publisher, NLP Trainer and Nurseryman.

Jack Stewart, BA, MSc, FCIPD, has spent most of his working life as a trainer and developer in the public, private and voluntary sectors. He has designed and run  training programmes, team building and other 'interventions' for thousands of directors, teachers, managers, children, supervisors and employees.

Through personal experience of leading change in local government, combined with his research interests, he co–authored 'The Learning Organization in the Public Services' published by Gower in 1997.

Since establishing Organisational Healing in 1995, Jack has diversified into running and franchising NLP (Neuro–Linguistic Programming) Practitioner and Master Practitioner courses. He has designed and run NLP–based programmes in schools (Modelling Genius, 'Re–righting the Code'). Twice he has addressed the annual Early Years conference organised by Walsall LEA. Working with David Miskimin means he can now help parents nationally and internationally.

Jack has a psychotherapy and coaching practice, and he published the personal development magazine the Magic Lamp, (now on–line), six years ago. He was a consultant to Shrewsbury Town Football Club, and Warrington Wolves Rugby League Club, helping players be more skilled at the mental side of the game.

Prior to 1995, Jack was a senior lecturer and CIPD examiner in personnel management, and taught strategic management for the Open University's MBA.

In September 2004, Jack co–produced with Jeff Moran the unique Purrfect Symphony CD. He is now developing his skills as a spiritual teacher, and his (about tenth at the last count) latest life change is to become the proud owner of a cottage nursery business.

Jack is married to Anne, and they have two daughters; Karen and Janet (stepdaughters to Jack) and three grandchildren; James, Nicola and Josh.

Jack can be contacted through email to jack@organisationalhealing.org.

Recommended Reading

RAPPORT

The Way of NLP, Joseph O'Connor and Ian Mc Dermott, *Thorsons, 2001.*

Influencing with Integrity by Genie Laborde, *Anglo–American Book Company 1987.*

NLP and Relationships, Robin Prior and Joseph O'Connor, *Thorsons, 2000.*

SELF–CONFIDENCE

No Ordinary Moments by Dan Millman, *H J Kramer Inc., 1992.*

Awaken the Giant Within by Anthony Robbins, *Simon & Schuster, 1992.*

The Self–Esteem Companion by McKay, Fanning, Honeychurch, Sutker, *New Harbinger Publications, 1999.*

Shift Happens by Robert Holden, *Hodder & Stoughton, 2000.*

LEARNING

Rediscovering the Joy of Learning by Don Blackerby, *Success Skills Inc. 1996.*

Brain Based Learning by Eric Jensen, *The Brain Store, 1995.*

Rhythms of Learning, Chris Brewer & Don G Campbell, *Zephyr Press, 1991.*

How to think like Leonardo da Vinci, Michael Gelb, *Thorsons, 1998.*

The five major pieces to the life puzzle, Jim Rohn, *Dickinson Press, 1991.*

Now, Discover Your Strengths, Buckingham M and Clifton DO, *Free Press, 2001.*

COACHING

Personal Coaching for Results by Lou Tice, *Thomas Nelson Publishers, 1997.*

Effective Coaching: Lessons from the Coaches' Coach, Myles Downey, *Texere Publishing, 2003.*

Coaching for Performance, John Whitmore, *Nicholas Brearley Publishing, 1997.*

Breaking the Rules: Removing the Obstacles to Effortless High Performance, Wright K, *CPM Publishers, 1998.*

Co–active Coaching: New Skills for Coaching People Toward Success in Work and Life, Whitworth, Kimsey–House and Sandahl, *Davies–Black Publishing, 1998.*

Living Your Best Life, Laura Berman Fortgang, *Jeremy P. , Tarcher/Putnam, 2002.*

OPTIMISING STRESS

The Power of Now by Eckhart Tolle, *Hodder & Stoughton, 2001.*

Purrfect Symphony and Relaxing with Cats CDs by Jeff Moran & Jack Stewart, both available from *www.purrfectsymphony.com*

The Power of Intention by Wayne W Dyer, *Hay House 2004.*

Services

THE DIRECTORS COACH

www.TheDirectorsCoach.com

The range of our services has grown steadily in line with market and client demands and we now provide a comprehensive framework for strengthening human resources. Effective career intervention, focused goal setting, coaching and mentoring are increasingly important facets of leadership and talent management, contributing to effective workplace strategies and better decision making. Currently we offer services addressing five key areas:

1. Organisational Coaching & Consultancy

2. Executive and Leadership Coaching

3. Team Development

4. Recruitment, Induction and Career Management

5. Employee Assistance Programme (EAP)

All of the above involve transitions. These occur every day for organisations and individuals: mergers and acquisitions, restructurings, promotions, downsizings, role transitions and retirements.

Transitions are major investments and demand high returns – usually step–changes in performance. Few deliver these results. Transitions are tough to get right because their success depends on people, and people are complex, emotional beings. Transitions are times of heightened emotions where small differences in what is done can lead to vast disparities in perception and performance.

Meeting the needs of those who leave the business and continuing to inspire high performance in those who remain, is challenging. Motivating and aligning employees with an organisation's business goals is a complex and uncertain process that can overwhelm even experienced leaders.

There are, however, tried and tested ways to help the transition of people and the organisations for which they work. Successful transitions can achieve outstanding results. We understand this at The Directors Coach.

If any of the above are of interest and you'd like to know more, we'd be pleased to hear from you.

The Directors Coach
44 Keats Lane
Wincham
Northwich
Cheshire
CW9 6PP
+44 (0) 1565 734 561

ORGANISATIONAL HEALING

www.OrganisationalHealing.org

Therapy and coaching
Jack has been helping psychotherapy and coaching clients for over 10 years. Helping you answer the question 'What do you want?' and allowing you to rise to levels beyond your expectations.

Group training
As a development consultant, Jack has helped dozens of organisations manage change. His strengths lie in personal development and team building programmes for small groups.

Transforming Disaffection
With sound therapist and presenter Jeff Moran, we work with schools, helping disaffected children and young adults who want to realise their potential.

Modelling
All learning is modelling, whether the model is a person, academic knowledge, or nature. Jack has been researching the modelling process for 5 years and has created practical techniques combining ancient and contemporary wisdom. Mastery of modelling will help you acquire all traits you admire in others.

Writing
Jack has co–authored two books, *The Learning Organisation in the Public Services* [Gower 1997], and *The Coaching Parent* [BookShaker.com 2005]. He is currently writing 3 more. *Moving for a Change* [personal change through movement] will be published by Bookshaker.com in 2006, *Modelling Life* [using modelling techniques to become who you want to be], and his autobiography, *Eowt Covers a Naked Mon*. He also edits the internet magazine, the *Rolling Lamp*.

PURRFECT SYMPHONY

www.PurrfectSymphony.com

Blending the science of sound with nature to relax, heal and energise. With Jeff Moran, two CD's have been created to date, Purrfect Symphony and Relax With Cats. More are planned, including a meditation CD.

BLUEBELL HEALING LODGE

www.BluebellHealingLodge.com

A healing retreat set in formal gardens and a plant nursery in rural Cheshire due to open in summer 2006.

Jack Stewart
Organisational Healing
7 Asher Court
Barley Castle Trading Estate
Appleton
Warrington
WA4 4ST
+44 (0) 1925 861 600

Index

Additional Learning Aids
For The Coaching Parent

Are you a parent, step–parent or grandparent? Do you work with or look after children? How often do you wonder if there really are enhanced ways of relating to them…?

If there was a better way of helping improve your child's life chances would you want to know? No matter what age you are now – whether as a parent or child, what would you do?

Buy the cards and CD to accompany
The Coaching Parent book by visiting:

www.thedirectorscoach.com

www.organisationalhealing.org

Bonus – Buy the cards and CD at the same time and receive an extra 15% discount

Your No–Risk, Money–Back Guarantee

If you buy the cards or CD and learn absolutely nothing, just send them back to us and we'll gladly refund your money. That's it – simple.

CPSIA information can be obtained at www.ICGtesting.com
231511LV00007B/25/A